Cars

DATE DUE

AUG 1 5 2007		
AUG 1 4 2008		
JUL 8 2015		

Demco, Inc. 38-293

Cars

EXAMINING POP CULTURE

DAVID M. HAUGEN AND MATTHEW J. BOX,
Book Editors

Bruce Glassman, Vice President

Bonnie Szumski, Publisher

Helen Cothran, Managing Editor

GREENHAVEN PRESS
An imprint of Thomson Gale, a part of The Thomson Corporation

THOMSON
GALE

Detroit • New York • San Francisco • San Diego • New Haven, Conn.
Waterville, Maine • London • Munich

10|04   #57134596

LIBRARY OF CONGRESS CATALOGING-IN-PUBLICATION DATA

Cars / David M. Haugen and Matthew J. Box, book editors.
p. cm.—(Examining pop culture)
Includes bibliographical references and index.
ISBN 0-7377-2543-5 (lib. : alk. paper)
1. Automobiles—Social aspects—United States—History. 2. Popular culture—United States. I. Haugen, David M., 1969– . II. Box, Matthew J. III. Series.
HE5623.C35 2005
303.48'32—dc22   2004060718

CONTENTS

Chapter 1: The Car's Impact on Society

Chapter 2: Car Cultures

Chapter 3: Cultural Myths and Symbols

POPULAR CULTURE IS THE COMMON SET OF ARTS, entertainments, customs, beliefs, and values shared by large segments of society. Russel B. Nye, one of the founders of the study of popular culture, wrote that "not until the appearance of mass society in the eighteenth century could popular culture, as one now uses the term, be said to exist." According to Nye, the Industrial Revolution and the rise of democracy in the eighteenth and nineteenth centuries led to increased urbanization and the emergence of a powerful middle class. In nineteenth-century Europe and North America, these trends created audiences for the popular arts that were larger, more concentrated, and more well off than at any point in history. As a result, more people shared a common culture than ever before.

The technological advancements of the twentieth century vastly accelerated the spread of popular culture. With each new advance in mass communication—motion pictures, radio, television, and the Internet—popular culture has become an increasingly pervasive aspect of everyday life.

Popular entertainment—in the form of movies, television, theater, music recordings and concerts, books, magazines, sporting events, video games, restaurants, casinos, theme parks, and other attractions—is one very recognizable aspect of popular culture. In his 1999 book *The Entertainment Economy: How Mega-Media Forces Are Transforming Our Lives*, Michael J. Wolf argues that entertainment is becoming the dominant feature of American society: "In choosing where we buy French fries, how we relate to political candidates, what airline we want to fly, what pajamas we choose for our kids, and which mall we want to buy them in, entertainment is increasingly influencing every one of those choices. . . . Multiply that by the billions of choices that, collectively, all of us make each day and you have a portrait of a society in which entertainment is one of its leading institutions."

It is partly this pervasive quality of popular culture that makes it worthy of study. James Combs, the author of *Polpop: Politics and Popular Culture in America*, explains that examining popular culture is important because it can shape people's attitudes and beliefs:

> Popular culture is so much a part of our lives that we cannot deny its developmental powers. . . . Like formal education or family rearing, popular culture is part of our "learning environment.". . . Though our pop culture education is informal—we usually do not attend to pop culture for its "educational" value—it nevertheless provides us with information and images upon which we develop our opinions and attitudes. We would not be what we are, nor would our society be quite the same, without the impact of popular culture.

Examining popular culture is also important because popular movies, music, fads, and the like often reflect popular opinions and attitudes. Christopher D. Geist and Jack Nachbar explain in *The Popular Culture Reader*, "the popular arts provide a gauge by which we can learn what Americans are thinking, their fears, fantasies, dreams, and dominant mythologies. The popular arts reflect the values of the multitude."

This two-way relationship between popular culture and society is evident in many modern discussions of popular culture. Does the glorification of guns by many rap artists, for example, merely reflect the realities of inner-city life, or does it also contribute to the problem of gun violence? Such questions also arise in discussions of the popular culture of the past. Did the Vietnam protest music of the late 1960s and early 1970s, for instance, simply reflect popular antiwar sentiments, or did it help turn public opinion against the war? Examining such questions is an important part of understanding history.

Greenhaven Press's *Examining Pop Culture* series provides students with the resources to begin exploring these questions. Each volume in the series focuses on a particular aspect of popular culture, with topics as varied as popular culture itself. Books in the series may focus on a particular genre, such as *Rap and Hip Hop*, while others may cover a specific medium, such as *Computers and the Internet*. Volumes such as *Body Piercing and Tattoos* have their focus on recent trends in popular culture, while titles like *Americans' Views About War* have a broader historical scope.

In each volume, an introductory essay provides a general

overview of the topic. The selections that follow offer a survey of critical thought about the subject. The readings in *Americans' Views About War*, for example, are arranged chronologically: Essays explore how popular films, songs, television programs, and even comic books both reflected and shaped public opinion about American wars from World War I through Vietnam. The essays in *Violence in Film and Television*, on the other hand, take a more varied approach: Some provide historical background, while others examine specific genres of violent film, such as horror, and still others discuss the current controversy surrounding the issue.

Each book in the series contains a comprehensive index to help readers quickly locate material of interest. Perhaps most importantly, each volume has an annotated bibliography to aid interested students in conducting further research on the topic. In today's culture, what is "popular" changes rapidly from year to year and even month to month. Those who study popular culture must constantly struggle to keep up. The volumes in Greenhaven's *Examining Pop Culture* series are intended to introduce readers to the major themes and issues associated with each topic, so they can begin examining for themselves what impact popular culture has on their own lives.

The Road to Conformity

IN AMERICA THE AUTOMOBILE IS THE ULTIMATE symbol of individual freedom. Cars afford people the mobility to reach nearly any chosen destination. Furthermore, auto travel allows drivers to set their own course, determine their own travel times, and start and stop at their convenience. Beyond these practical freedoms, automobiles also reflect their owners' individual sense of style and sense of self. Street racers and car customizers, for example, turn their vehicles into personal, artistic statements that reveal a worship of design or speed and set the owners apart or liberate them from the banalities of possessing yet another family sedan or common sports car. But even those who purchase the multitudes of factory-built automobiles tend to impose their personalities upon their vehicles. Sloganeering bumper stickers, rearview mirror trinkets, dashboard icons, and chrome wheel rims are but a few of the common fixtures that drivers use to individualize their autos and project their personality. The automobile thus embodies America's restless pioneer spirit coupled with the freedom of individual expression. And as such it has come to be, in the words of authors Frank Coffey and Joseph Layden, "the central object of American culture."[1]

All these notions of freedom and individuality, however, have often overshadowed the fact that the automobile is also an agent of conformity in America. Nearly every car is built in a similar manner, under similar factory specifications, and this has resulted—especially in the later part of the twentieth century—in fleets of vehicles that look nearly identical. Beyond the construction and appearance of the automobile, though, the creation of a car culture in America has also led to conformity in society itself. For example, road networks have made metropolitan regions across the country appear almost identical. And the individual roadside franchises that spring up in one area are designed to look similar to the ones in other locales so that drivers can identify them with ease. Thus, the much-touted "freedom of the open road" has lost some of its meaning in the late twentieth and early twenty-first centuries. For if the automobile ever offered the limitless possibilities of travel and escape, today's driver has more or less the option of motoring from one paved community (with its attendant, car-friendly strip malls) to another nearly identical community at the other end of the highway.

From Unique Playthings to Standardized Commodities

While the conformity inspired or even engendered by the automobile may seem to correspond with social trends in America's late-twentieth-century mass culture, the origins can be traced almost as far back as the advent of gasoline-powered transport in the United States. Auto engineering began in Europe and migrated across the Atlantic in the late nineteenth century. Two bicycle makers, Charles E. Duryea and his brother Frank, are commonly credited with building the first gasoline-powered vehicle in America in 1893. With a maiden voyage that traversed only two hundred feet of Massachusetts countryside, the Duryeas' horseless carriage heralded a great change in society. From that point on, scores of early mechanics and visionaries would become the nation's pioneer automakers. By 1900 there were at least one hundred carmakers in the United States, each producing handmade gasoline- and electric-powered buggies. The country was on its way to creating a motorized society.

Before the great change could take place, however, the automobile had to become a commodity within the reach of a majority of American households. Initially the car was a toy of the wealthy. Small production numbers and handcraftsmanship kept early auto prices high. The first cars were status symbols. The owners were set apart from the masses not only by their wealth but also by the uniqueness of their transportation. In an era when most Americans still relied on horsepower, the car owners could zip into town in their clanking runabouts, scaring horses, chasing pedestrians off the streets, and generally making their presence known. To the general public, then, early cars were at best a curiosity and at worst a nuisance. Those who could afford them were either castigated for the disruptions they caused or idolized for the interest they generated.

Regardless of the problems cars seemed to cause, by the turn of the century Americans' fascination with automobiles was definitely growing. Still, most people could only dream of motoring along the open road at an exhilarating twenty miles per hour. The car had yet to leave the clutches of the well-to-do. In 1901, however, one automaker opened the door to widespread car ownership. After a fire destroyed his small car-manufacturing shop in Detroit, Michigan, a young enthusiast named Ransom Olds concluded that in order to resurrect his finances and stay in the auto business, he would have to make and sell more cars than his competition. To accomplish this, he decided to abolish the system of building vehicles with unique handmade parts and, instead, to develop generic, interchangeable parts that could be used to manufacture identical automobiles. He also contracted with other manufacturers to supply standardized engines, transmissions, and bodies for his new fleet of vehicles. In effect, Olds turned his rebuilt auto plant into an automobile construction operation that could generate one look-alike Oldsmobile after another. Olds was thus the first to make the automobile conform to a specific appearance—one dictated by the standardization of its parts.

Fordism

With assembly line production, Olds was able to drop the prices of his autos to $650, a price within the reach of many working-class Americans. But Ransom Olds was not alone in embracing the new production methods afforded by interchangeable parts. Henry Ford, an auto racer and disgruntled former employee of two Detroit car manufacturers, banked on creating an auto empire that would use prefabricated parts tailored to Ford's own vehicle designs. In 1902 he opened the Ford Motor Company, a small plant that merely assembled cars from components shipped from outside contractors. "The way to make automobiles," Ford told one of his investors, "is to make one automobile just like another automobile, to make them all alike, to make them come through the factory alike—just like one pin is like another pin when it comes from the pin factory, or like one match is like another match when it comes from the match factory."[2] In this manner Ford created his Model A in 1904 and offered it to the public for $850.

Never content with his production quotas, Ford toyed with another manufacturing method in 1908. Working on his Model N car, Ford had his work-ers lay out the constituent parts of each car in a path along the floor of his machine shop. The body of each car had its axles and wheels put on at the head of this pathway and then the bulk was rolled along to each successive station where the nearby parts were added to the vehicle. At the end of the path a complete Model N would exit the plant and await distribution to a car dealer. His experiment was a primitive assembly line. It would not be until 1913, however, that Ford would install moving assem-bly lines in his factory that would automatically shunt the cars

Henry Ford

along to each workstation and result in production rates of mil-lions of vehicles per year. These assembly lines not only en-forced the conformity of the autos that moved along them, but they also brought about conformity in the workplace. Machin-ists specialized in specific tasks and became cogs in the larger mechanism of the automated factory. Those who failed to fit in with the mechanism could be replaced. Those who conformed to the system performed regimented jobs and earned preset wages determined by the skill involved in their given tasks. Fordism, as these mass production techniques were initially dubbed, determined work hours, wages, and production. Other automakers had to implement these methods or risk being shut out of the market.

Ford's new mass production methods were designed to cre-ate his motor company's ultimate contribution to automobile history—the Model T car. Inaugurated in 1908, the Model T was the realization of Henry Ford's proclamation that he would "build a motorcar for the multitudes."[3] It was a four-cylinder automobile with a simple, efficient design. The Model T ran well, but its elementary construction meant that if it broke down, it could easily be repaired—often by the untrained owner. Its dependability became its selling point. For nearly a decade the Model T dominated the auto market, and its $850 price tag (which declined over successive years) enticed many Americans to partake of the personal freedom that the automobile offered. In 1927, the last year of the Model T's production, the cost of the vehicle had dropped to only $290. By then, 15 million had been sold.

Emancipator and Equalizer

The reliable and resilient Ford auto gave Americans the ability to travel much farther and much faster than they could by horse or foot. This allowed city dwellers the opportunity to relocate outside the confines of urban manufacturing centers and motor to work from suburban homes. It also permitted rural drivers to reach towns and cities where everything from shopping to entertainment to cultural events was accessible. Furthermore, the automobile gave individuals the means to reach other destinations—across the country, if they so desired—that were previously beyond the realm of practical possibility. Frank Coffey and Joseph Layden state, "Because of its availability, the Model T was instrumental in reshaping American society. . . . To many people it was nothing less than the great emancipator."[4]

However, this freedom had other consequences. Once the automobile was in the hands of more than just the idle rich, it became "an equalizer, capable of breaking down, at least temporarily, any number of social and economic barriers."[5] The intermixing of rural and urban populations as well as the intermingling of regional populations meant that country folk became less distinguishable from their urban counterparts. Farmers dressed in city clothes could pass for businessmen in any metropolis, and their children, who could now reach better schools, received the same education as the children of urban parents. News of current events reached rural areas with greater speed thanks to the automobile, and even such seemingly inconsequential news as the buzz about popular motion picture stars became part of a shared national culture. America therefore became a bit more cosmopolitan as a result of widespread automobile use.

The Car Culture Develops

To facilitate the mobility of an increasing number of drivers, cities and states needed to improve their road networks. Still geared toward the horse and carriage, most American thoroughfares were uneven, rutted dirt paths. In addition, many well-traveled roads were only wide enough to accommodate one wagon or other conveyance; only city streets were designed to handle more traffic. As early as 1896, when auto making was in its infancy, urban planners and researchers theorized that paved roadways would encourage horseless transportation, which would ease traffic congestion caused by slow and ponderous carts and eliminate the horse manure and other wastes that made city streets unclean and unsafe. In1899 an article from *Harper's Weekly* opined, "a good many folks to whom every horse is a wild beast feel much safer on a machine than behind a quadruped, who has a mind of his own, and emotions which may not always be forestalled or controlled."[6] Some cities like Detroit (home of the auto giants) began paving some roads with asphalt or concrete before 1910, but it was not until just after World War I that the federal government stepped in to nationalize part of the process. In 1921 federal lawmakers, pressured by military interests who argued that better roads were vital to national security, passed the first Federal Highway Act. This law financed the resurfacing or repair of several major arteries that connected cities across the nation.

As the highways improved and travelers began taking trips farther from home, businesses that catered to motorists sprang up across the map in the 1920s. Fast-food restaurants, motor inns, gas stations, and auto camps appeared in most major towns and cities and even in sparsely populated areas where travelers were likely to stop. Many of these early roadside ventures were mom-and-pop operations that struggled to lure customers away from competition just down the road. Since most offered similar products (e.g., all drive-in restaurants concentrated on selling hamburgers and other foods that required little preparation), these establishments tried to entice customers by developing a unique image. Some created unusual signage, others offered arresting decor or architecture (such as buildings shaped like animals or Native American tepees), and still others worked to provide expedient service. Tourists were treated to genuinely novel experiences as they made their way to their ultimate destinations. Motoring was, in fact, its own adventure.

This Year's Model

Just as many roadside businesses of the 1920s aimed at originality to differentiate themselves from their competition, car manufacturers also strove for novelty. Americans in the Jazz Age were looking for excitement, and the plain, boxy Model T did not seem to capture the spirit of the era. Henry Ford initially failed to note the changing tastes of car buyers, and his "motorcar for the multitudes" fell out of favor. Other carmakers, such as Packard, Hudson, and Studebaker, however, were there to satisfy Ford's ex-customers. These new industry giants offered more than just reliable transportation; they produced sleek and sophisticated-looking status symbols. Their automobiles were more expensive than the Model T, but the post–World War I stock market boom made Americans feel flush with cash. Car buyers demanded speed and luxury, and manufacturers began marketing their latest autos as faster and more splendid than last year's models. Ford eventually caught on to the trend in 1927 when his company released the Model A, a more elegant roadster, to compete with his adversaries.

The auto industry, along with most American businesses, entered a slump when the Great Depression of the 1930s crippled the stock market and nearly everyone's personal finances. While most people could not afford to buy a new car, they did hold on to their old ones. Only after the nation became involved in World War II did the industry get back on its feet. Yet while the robust wartime economy cured the ills of the Depression, it forced Detroit automakers to switch to military production. Car production ceased during the war, but the companies gained by greatly increasing their manufacturing capabilities and learning how to work with new materials—such as stronger metals, plastics, and glass—that would find their way into automobiles in the postwar years. When the war did end in 1945, Detroit quickly retooled and pushed out new car designs within two years. And returning servicemen, who joined the lingering industrial boom, had the money to spend on whatever the automakers delivered—as long as it was new.

The juggernaut of American wartime industry—exemplified by the car manufacturers—transformed the national economy in the mid-1940s. Mass production provided an enormous variety of products to choose from. Advertising touted these products as necessary elements of the American dream—items that saved time and labor and made life more pleasant for those who could afford them. Automobiles were the centerpiece of the postwar dream, and many Americans had to have a new one every few years to ensure (and reveal to others) that they were indeed living the good life. The auto industry skyrocketed as sales improved, and, as automotive historian Ron Edsforth explains, all the industries that supplied the auto industry boomed along with it, creating "the greatest prosperity in American history."[7]

The 1950s Consumer Society

As the nation embraced its prosperity, three automakers came to dominate the industry. Ford, Chrysler, and General Motors sold the lion's share of vehicles and determined the standards of car design and function. At the dawn of the 1950s the Big Three created wildly inviting concepts that included vivid color schemes, curvaceous body contours, chrome trim, and prominent but utterly useless tail fins. The public eagerly bought each new variation, and the postwar consumer society—in which acquiring the latest innovation to keep pace with what other Americans were buying—was born. Thirty or forty years earlier, car buyers based their buying decisions on practical factors such as the speed of the engine or the steering mode. In the 1950s, however, car buyers were more influenced by cosmetic features. Advertisers pushed design and style as the differentiating factors. And while in previous decades the car was a unique status symbol because it was still a complete luxury for most, by the 1950s the majority of Americans owned at least one car. Thus, for members of the expansive and influential middle class, buying the latest, sleekest-looking automobile did not show that the owner had gained new social status; rather, it indicated that he or she was still part of the middle class.

Catering to the new car-oriented citizens of the 1950s was a new crop of car-oriented businesses. Unlike the mom-and-pop establishments or small chain diners and motels that took root in the 1920s, 1950s roadside enterprises were dominated by the concept of franchising. In 1954, for example, a milk shake machine salesman named Ray Kroc was captivated by the success of a small chain of California drive-in restaurants run by the McDonald brothers, Richard and Maurice. The Mc-Donalds had built a handful of fast-food restaurants that served only ten items, all of which could be prepared very quickly to meet the needs of the busy clientele. These items included hamburgers, French fries, and milk shakes—foods that would come to define the fast-food industry in years to come. Kroc worked out a franchising agreement with the brothers so that he could license the name and concept of McDonald's drive-ins to interested entrepreneurs in other locations across the country. The trademark "golden arches" were designed by Richard McDonald in 1953, and the first franchise to use this symbol appeared in Arizona that year. The whole venture took off quickly, and within two years Kroc was able to buy up the original chain from the McDonald brothers. Other fast-food chains followed suit, and eventually drive-ins such as Bob's Big Boy, Steak 'N Shake, and A&W dotted many regions of the country. Each offered a limited menu—often containing the same food items that could be found in any competing franchise.

Uniformity of Roadside Commercial Strips

As the example of McDonald's illustrates, franchisers not only bought the concept and product from the original operation, they also bought signage, an identifiable architecture, and similar promotional materials. The purpose of these image-making elements was to create customer loyalty by enhancing recognition. Franchise-specific signs, character icons, and architecture made these establishments instantly identifiable to passing motorists. Their purpose was to draw drivers off the highway.

Once certain off-ramp locations became popular, other businesses aggregated around the successful franchise. Many of these latecomers were franchises, too. Dunkin' Donuts, Midas Mufflers, and Century-21 real estate brokers were but a few of the recognizable chains that cropped up in off-ramp communities. Eventually such commercial strips appeared along the outskirts of every major city and town, and people flocked to them because they could be sure—thanks to franchise recognition—of what products and services they would find there. "Security and sameness were what the franchises offered," Christopher Finch writes, "and whether one likes it or not, it was what the American public wanted."[8] Americans wanted to rely on the product and service standards that they believed were upheld in franchise businesses. The establishments of past decades had striven for uniqueness in appearance, but new chains advocated the safety of sameness.

The Paving of America

The off-ramp commercial cluster did, as the name implies, require the off-ramp. As in the 1920s, the national government stepped in to improve interstate highways in the mid-1950s when it was apparent that the older road networks would be strained by the dramatic rise in automobile ownership. In 1956 President Dwight Eisenhower signed the Interstate Highway Act, which used mainly federal revenues to underwrite the construction of forty-one thousand miles of cross-country superhighways. These multilane ribbons of concrete were wider than their predecessors, and they had ten-foot-wide shoulders, few gradients, and gentle curves—all of which helped traffic keep moving. From the outset the new highways were designed to blend in with the surroundings. Especially near large communities, engineers made the effort to keep the road profile from intruding on the landscape, and businesses as well as billboards were kept at a distance so as not to entice drivers to slow down. The commercial districts were, instead, centered at the highway exit ramps, where traffic could resume a leisurely pace on stop-and-go surface streets.

While the superhighway engineers tried to incorporate aesthetics into their planning, the road networks came to define the landscape instead of vanishing into it. Most American cities viewed from above have identical features—perpendicular sets of major arteries, bypasses, business loops, and numerous cloverleaf on- and off-ramps. The highways dictate where business centers will arise and where urban decay will be contained, and this has done much to make one metropolitan area look very much like another. City interiors and their suburbs have also developed similar appearances in response to the dominance of the automobile since the 1950s. Green spaces and parkways have disappeared, and parking spaces, parking lots, and other paved areas have taken their place. "City by city, suburb by suburb, we have a hard-topped nation," writes architecture critic Jane Holtz Kay. "From 30 to 50 percent of urban America is given over to the car, two-thirds in Los Angeles. In Houston the figure for the amount of asphalt is 30 car spaces per resident."[9] The needs of the motorist (primarily the need to easily navigate dense, urban environments and the ability to park at any destination) became the imperative of urban planners, and this focus on the car culture completely reshaped every American city.

Suburban Sameness

Besides changing the face of urban areas, the automobile also gave rise to suburbia. Although flight from inner-city neighborhoods began in the 1910s and 1920s when automobiles gave city workers the opportunity to live some distance from their jobs, the heyday of the suburban subdivision was the 1950s and 1960s. As Frank Coffey and Joseph Layden note, "The suburban population in the United States increased by nearly 50 percent in the 1950s, changing forever the way Americans lived and worked."[10] It was highway construction that prompted the mass emigration from crowded urban areas. Improved travel times on modern highways meant that workers could live farther and farther from city centers.

Several planned suburban communities sprouted up overnight on undeveloped land or former farm pastures that were once considered rural, but now had become part of greater metropolitan areas. Many of these suburbs were laid out in similar grid patterns with housing lots divided up into one- or two-acre parcels. The most famous and imitated were the subdivisions created by William Levitt in vacant areas of Long Island, New York. Levittowns, as these suburbs were called, were constructed at a rate of forty houses per day. All the homes were based on the same floor plan and were arranged in neat rows that fronted broad avenues. The grid of avenues generally defined the current limits of the suburb. Following the maze of streets, a resident could eventually reach the highway on-ramp to speed off to work or shop in other parts of the metropolitan area. Americans who could afford to embrace these cookie-cutter homesteads because the alternative—staying in crowded, polluted urban environments—was undesirable and unnecessary. As author and editor James Howard Kunstler remarks, "For many, it was a vast improvement over what they were used to. The houses were spacious compared to city dwellings, and they contained modern conveniences. Air, light, and a modicum of greenery came with the package." But as Kunstler concludes, "The main problem with it was that it dispensed with all the traditional connections and continuities of community life, and replaced them with little more than cars and television."[11]

Changing Times

In the mid-1950s the Big Three automakers were catering to affluent, middle-class America by adding more luxury to their cars. Each model was a sculptured mass of steel and chrome that needed a huge, gas-guzzling engine just to propel the extra weight of fins, a hardtop roof, and flashy trim. A slight recession in 1957, however, heralded a change in trends. Bulky cars that got five miles to the gallon became a liability. While the majority of middle-class Americans were reluctant to give up their chrome dream machines, a growing number began turning to economical alternatives. By the beginning of the 1960s the gap was filled by foreign cars. Smaller and less stylish, autos manufactured primarily in Germany and Japan proved to be reliant, efficient, and affordable. Some Americans chose them as perfect second cars for busy, on-the-go families. Detroit took heed of the trend and started to produce compact cars, though not at the expense of its luxury lines.

Then, in 1965 American carmakers were forced to seriously rethink American automotive design. In that year a lawyer and consumer advocate named Ralph Nader published *Unsafe at Any Speed: The Designed-in Dangers of the American Automobile*. The best-selling book took American automakers to task for failing to make safety the primary consideration of new cars.

The result, Nader claimed, was the production of many dangerous vehicles that accounted for untold numbers of highway accidents each year. The public outcry was great, and the Big Three could not ignore it.

What contributed to the popularity of Nader's argument, however, was not merely his message, but the temper of the times. The 1960s witnessed radical challenges to the status quo as established and usually unquestioned bastions of authority came under scrutiny. Some came to realize that perhaps the revered automakers in Detroit did not have consumers' best interests at heart. Chief among the converts was the generation of young people who came of age in the 1950s. The children of middle-class suburbia swelled the ranks that called for change in the 1960s. Having lived the good life, they suddenly turned on suburban values and chastised suburbia for its smugness and isolation. The youth movement became especially concerned about the nation that they would inherit. Young people began fighting for such issues as social justice, civil liberties, and environmental protection. It was the latter cause that related directly to the automobile. By the beginning of the decade, scientists had already linked automobile emissions to the problem of smog that had polluted many of America's largest cities. Not willing to appear unconcerned, automakers fashioned exhaust controls and implemented smaller, fuel-efficient engines to reduce excess emissions. It was one of the first signs that Detroit was no longer dictating changes in auto design but was actually responding to the concerns of the car buyers.

The Gas Crunch

At the beginning of the 1970s, the young and socially conscious generation became a larger segment of the car-buying public. While some desired the speed and image of Detroit's powerful muscle cars, others opted for foreign cars or American compact automobiles that were cheaper and more economical to operate. In fact, it was the economy of the smaller car that eventually made it the focus of auto making in the new decade (and from then onward). The instigating factor in this great change was the oil crisis of 1973 and 1974, when Arab oil-producing countries raised petroleum prices in response to U.S. support for Israel during the Yom Kippur War. While it is debatable whether there was ever a shortage of gasoline in America at that time, prices at the pump shot up and caused panic. By the end of 1973 sales of compact cars caught up with those of bigger models.

The nation that came out on top of the oil crisis was Japan. Having built economy cars for some time, Japanese corporations like Mazda, Subaru, Toyota, and Honda had already mastered compact engineering. By the mid-1970s they were working on style. In 1976 Honda released its Accord, and the impact was immediate. The Accord was a luxury midsize car that had fuel efficiency, a relatively powerful engine, and the attractive look of a smartly designed vehicle. It offered everything in one package—something no U.S. (or even European) automobile could match. But the post-1973 gasoline prices forced American automakers to follow the Japanese lead or suffer decline. American midsize and compact car production quickly outpaced their luxury counterparts. "After 1973," Christopher Finch concludes, "many Americans began to play by the same rules as Asians and Europeans, and with this came the sameness of product that afflicts the automobile marketplace today."[12]

Ford Revisited

After the oil scare of the 1970s, economy was the foremost concern of most new auto buyers. As a result, American manufacturers replaced steel bodies with lightweight metals and plastic, which translated into greater fuel efficiency. Practical contours and a lack of chrome accoutrements also removed excess weight and aided aerodynamics. Safety concerns were now also a priority for carmakers. Whatever innovations in economy and safety one company's design team implemented was sure to be copied by all other car manufacturers.

Fierce competition from the Japanese—who, from the 1980s on, dominated car sales worldwide—also meant that American carmakers could not afford to experiment as wildly as in the past. To be sure, atypical car designs persisted, but they were the exception, and their price tags usually put them beyond the means of many American families. Even as the economy improved, attitudes did not change radically. As the less-fuel-efficient sport-utility vehicles, for example, came onto the market, their individual designs were dictated by the same practical concerns that were now an entrenched part of Detroit's philosophy. Thus safety, gas mileage, and even the proposed use of the vehicle ended up making most of this new breed of automobiles look nearly identical. Ford's dream of producing a standardized auto that most of the public could afford has gone beyond the limits of a single manufacturer and become the operative procedure for the entire industry.

Notes

1. Frank Coffey and Joseph Layden, *America on Wheels: The First 100 Years: 1896–1996.* Los Angeles: General Publishing Group, 1996, p. 9.
2. Quoted in James J. Flink, *The Automobile Age.* Cambridge, MA: MIT Press, 1988, p. 43.
3. Quoted in Coffey and Layden, *America on Wheels*, p. 39.
4. Coffey and Layden, *America on Wheels*, p. 41.
5. Coffey and Layden, *America on Wheels*, p. 44.
6. Quoted in James J. Flink, *The Car Culture.* Cambridge, MA: MIT Press, 1975, p. 36.
7. Quoted in Coffey and Layden, *America on Wheels*, p. 141.
8. Christopher Finch, *Highways to Heaven: The Auto Biography of America.* New York: HarperCollins, 1992, p. 242.
9. Jane Holtz Kay, *Asphalt Nation: How the Automobile Took over America, and How We Can Take It Back.* New York: Crown, 1997, p. 64.
10. Coffey and Layden, *America on Wheels*, p. 173.
11. James Howard Kunstler, *The Geography of Nowhere: The Rise and Decline of America's Man-Made Landscape.* New York: Touchstone, 1993, p. 105.
12. Finch, *Highways to Heaven*, p. 319.

CHAPTER

1

The Car's Impact on Society

The Advent of the Automobile Transforms Rural and Urban Spaces

Joseph Interrante

In the following article Joseph Interrante explains how
the automobile helped change the urban and rural
space in America. According to Interrante, from the
advent of the mass-marketed Ford Model T in 1908
through the 1920s, cars gained in popularity with
Americans, and their affordability made them a commodity within reach of even the urban working class
and struggling rural farmers. With so many people
buying and using cars, traveling times shrank, and journeys that would have taken days by horseback could
now be accomplished in a matter of hours. Suddenly,
isolated farmers could reach towns and cities more easily, and urban laborers could move farther away from
the crowded industrial centers where they worked. As
Interrante elucidates, this freedom of movement im-
pacted living patterns (as suburbs grew outside cities)
as well as urban and rural economies (as shopping districts became centralized for the motorists' convenience). As these changes took place, Interrante argues,
Americans became trapped into a dependence on cars,
and the nation became a true car culture.

When this article was published, Joseph Interrante was a doctoral candidate at Harvard University

■

Joseph Interrante, "The Road to Autopia: The Automobile and the Spatial Transformation of the American Culture," *The Automobile and American Culture*, edited by
David L. Lewis and Laurence Goldstein. Ann Arbor: University of Michigan Press,
1983. Copyright © 1980 by The University of Michigan. All rights reserved. Reproduced by permission.

writing a dissertation entitled "A Moveable Feast: The Automobile and the Spatial Transformation of American Culture, 1890–1940."

IN THE 1920s, ROBERT AND HELEN LYND, IN THEIR classic study *Middletown*, found that the automobile had become "an accepted essential of normal living." It had become the primary focal point of urban family life, and had made leisure activity a customary aspect of everyday experience. Indeed, the car had become so important to Middletown residents that many families expressed a willingness to go without food and shelter, to mortgage their homes and deplete their bank savings, rather than lose their cars. "We'd rather do without clothes than give up the car," a working-class mother of nine told the Lynds. "I'll go without food before I'll see us give up the car," another wife said emphatically. Other observers found that rural families were similarly attached to their cars. When a farm woman was asked by a U.S. Department of Agriculture inspector during the 1920s why her family had purchased an automobile before equipping their home with indoor plumbing, she replied, "Why, you can't go to town in a bathtub!" For these urban and rural Americans alike, the car had become a basic social necessity. . . .

When the automobile first appeared as a mass-produced commodity after Henry Ford's introduction of the Model T in 1908, people bought automobiles because they met old transportation needs better than existing alternatives and offered new possibilities for movement. But use of the car also altered urban and rural life in important ways. . . . These changes were part of a general reorganization of the physical and social urban and rural environments which changed people's needs for transportation. . . .

Decentralized Economy

Between 1900 and 1940, changes in the structure of business enterprise and the strategy of industrial and market relations drastically transformed economic life in general and the urban economy in particular. Business firms extended their existing lines of goods to a greater number of customers at home, sought new markets and sources of materials overseas, and created new markets by developing new products for different kinds of customers. The expansion and diversification of markets occurred through the combination and consolidation of firms into single multidivisional corporations like E.I. DuPont, General Motors, and Sears, Roebuck and Company. These corporations were distinguished from older industrial firms by their integrated structures and coordinated functions. Decisions and information flowed through a hierarchy consisting of a general office, divisional offices, departmental headquarters, and field units. Changes in business structure, which were designed to plan effectively for long-term and short-term market exigencies and to insure an undisrupted flow of production for those markets, substantially altered, in turn, the quality of industrial work experience. A new class of professional and managerial workers was distributed among the various strata of the corporation to transmit instructions and information and to supervise directly the work process. . . .

Paradoxically, as multidivisional corporations integrated industrial and business relations, the spatial organization of manufacturing became decentralized. Corporations began to establish factories outside major urban centers in "industrial satellite cities" like Gary, Hammond, and East Chicago outside Chicago; Lackawanna outside Buffalo; East St. Louis and Alton across the Mississippi River from St. Louis; and Chester and Norristown near Philadelphia. Industrial growth in these satellite cities occurred at a faster rate than central city manufacturing: between 1899 and 1909, employment in the outlying districts around cities grew by 97.7 percent, while central city employment increased only 40.8 percent. . . .

Many residents displaced by the reorganization of economic activity and urban real estate within the city moved to outlying districts. This "suburban" boom, which began after World War I, peaked during the 1920s, and slowed but did not disappear during the 1930s, was based upon car travel. It was not simply an accelerated version of late nineteenth- and early twentieth-century streetcar movement into suburbs. Unrestricted by a need for access to mass transit facilities, real estate speculators located subdivisions everywhere around the central city. By 1922, 135,000 suburban homes in 60 cities were already wholly dependent upon cars for transportation. Most of these suburbanites were wealthy families, but during the 1920s and 1930s the movement out of the central city expanded to include the middle class (who located in exclusively residential suburbs) and the working class (who located closer to work in industrial suburbs). These outlying districts together grew during the 1920s at a rate twice as fast as the cities around which they were located. Even though the rate of increase slowed during the depression years, it remained impressive when contrasted with the absolute decline of population in central cities during the same period. By 1940, 13 million people lived in communities beyond the reach of public transportation.

Moreover, the socio-economic relationship between suburbs and the central city changed. As downtown shopping districts were transformed into central government and corporate headquarters, small retail services—which could not afford skyrocketing rents and were losing customers unwilling to face downtown traffic snarls—relocated in the suburbs near their customers. (One Atlanta drugstore owner, forced out of business in 1926, lamented, "The place where trade is, is where automobiles go. . . . A central location is no longer a good one for my sort of business.") Likewise, large department stores set up branch stores in these satellite communities. Mail-order firms like Sears, Roebuck and Montgomery Ward turned into suburban chains. Banks also established branches in suburbs. Dentists and doctors opened offices near their clients' (and their own) homes. In short, many formerly centralized institutions and services were relocated outside cities. These outlying districts became the retail business centers of urban space—especially in smaller cities which had never developed extensive trolley networks. Indeed, the Hoover Commission noted in 1933 that the old "star" pattern of nineteenth century urban development (a star whose rays ran along streetcar tracks) had been transformed into a veritable "constellation" of interdependent centers within a single metropolitan region. And the National Resources Committee declared in 1937 that the whole east coast from New York to Philadelphia had become a single "conurbanized" band of metropolitan settlement.

The dispersion of manufacturing and residential settlement was based upon car travel. The importance of the automobile varied, it is true, with the size of the city and the availability of public transportation. But even in cities with elaborate mass transit systems, like Boston, Chicago, Philadelphia, and New York, observers in the 1920s and 1930s noted that car travel was necessary for much of the business and recreation which took place in and around them. Moreover, the car's importance increased as streetcar service declined through mismanagement, overextension of services, and competition from jitneys and buses. Indeed, planners in these cities were deliberately reshaping the central city landscape by the late 1920s and 1930s in order to facilitate commutation by car. In these large cities, cars accounted for 20 to 32 percent of the daily traffic into the central business district (CBD) by 1930. Cars became more important earlier in smaller cities like Kansas City, Milwaukee, and Washington, D.C. There car travel during the 1920s accounted for 50 to 66 percent of the daily commutation into the CBD. By 1930, 222 cities with at least 10,000 residents were entirely dependent on motor transportation.

Urban space was enlarged through automobile use. The further one lived from the city, the more advantageous car travel became. A 1930 traffic control study of Kansas City illustrated the savings in time during the evening "rush hour." In the downtown area, trolleys and cars moved bumper to bumper. But outside the CBD, the car rapidly moved ahead of streetcars. Two miles from the CBD it had gained a five-minute advantage; at 7½ miles, it had gained 15 minutes. Along secondary trolley lines, on which service was less frequent, cars traversed the 7½ miles with a 35 minute advantage over streetcars. The same advantages were documented in Detroit in 1930. In addition to this daily flow of traffic into the city, automobiles made possible crosscurrents of movement throughout the outlying district— something streetcars could not do. In Los Angeles, this movement superseded commutation into the downtown area. The number of people entering downtown Los Angeles between 1923 and 1931 declined by 24 percent despite a population boom in the metropolitan area. But the most important point was that the reorganization of urban space made these crosscurrents of movement not only more possible but more necessary as well. Goods which families had purchased in old downtown shopping districts now had to be purchased at stores scattered throughout the suburbs. Many employees had to drive to decentralized workplaces, or from decentralized residences to the CBD. If the automobile first appeared as a convenience which permitted more frequent, faster, and more flexible transportation movement, metropolitanism[1] gradually made that movement an inescapable feature of urban living.

A Rural Necessity

As metropolitanism reoriented urban areas, it also reorganized rural space. But while the distinguishing characteristic of urban metropolitanism was decentralization, the principal transformation of rural space was a centralization of institutions and activity. Moreover, rural society was affected earlier and more deeply than urban society, in part because farmers bought Tin Lizzies sooner and in greater numbers than urban residents during the prewar period. In 1910, 0.17 percent of farm families owned 0.50 percent of the 450,000 registered motor vehicles in the United States; by 1930, 53.1 percent of the rural population owned 50.3 percent of the nation's 23 million cars. The reorganization of rural space which widespread car ownership facilitated changed farmers' needs for transportation. Within the specific context of those changes, the automobile was transformed from a rural convenience into a rural necessity.

From the 1890s through the farm depression of the 1920s and 1930s, the growth of large-scale agriculture, the use of tractors for field work, and the collapse of many mid-sized farms brought about a new rural economy. . . .

At the same time, the spatial organization of society changed. Many families who lost their farms and did not sink into tenancy or migrant labor moved, not to cities, but to rural villages and towns. Between 1920 and 1930, these towns gained 3.6 million people while the farm population decreased by 1.2 million. Furthermore, farm villages changed in socio-economic operation. Small crossroads centers lost their general trade and service functions to neighboring towns; some disappeared, while others became specialized agricultural supply depots. Small towns located on highways developed facilities catering to

---

1. the reconfigurement of urban, suburban, and rural relationships in light of society's adoption of the car as the primary means of transporatation

tourist traffic. Many formerly localized institutions and services—education, health care, postal service, general stores—and other formerly urban institutions—libraries, chain stores, gas stations—were relocated in and around the larger rural villages. These larger villages became the centers of rural space.

Rural space was not so much enlarged with automobile use as it was reshaped into a centralized and hierarchical form. Studies of automobile travel support this conclusion. Although rural people could travel greater distances with cars, most trips occurred within a previously demarcated local area. Studies of rural villages in 28 states in 1924–1930 found that the socioeconomic hinterland of two-thirds of them did not expand by as much as two square miles. And studies of car travel in five states between 1926 and 1928 found that one-third to one-half of all automobile trips measured under 20 miles. This was the approximate distance of a horse and wagon, but cars took less time to traverse it. Automobile use encouraged not longer trips, but more frequent ones. Families that traveled to a nearby village only one or two times per year before the car, traveled every three or four weeks with one. . . .

As in the urban case, the most important point was that the reorganization of rural space gradually made this movement both more possible and more necessary. Goods which the family had purchased at a crossroads store or by mail order now had to be purchased in town. (Mail-order houses . . . were turning into department chains.) This centralization of services in rural areas was part of metropolitan organization. Metropolitanism changed the structure of rural society so fundamentally that by the Depression a family without a car faced special difficulties in satisfying its transportation needs: it took longer to reach relocated services in village centers by horse and wagon; and barns, liveries, harness shops, and blacksmiths had dwindled as their owners converted them into auto dealerships, garages, gas stations, and parking lots. As a result of these and similar changes, the car became a rural necessity. . . .

Impact on Consumption and Women's Lives

In the 1920s, metropolitanism began to change household activity and consumption habits by drawing women out of the household and into the marketplace. Robert and Helen Lynd observed in their study of *Middletown* (1929): "The great bulk of the things consumed by American families is no longer made in the home and the efforts of family members are focused instead on buying a living." Middletown families bought more canned and prepared goods as well as fresh fruit and vegetables, more premade sweets, more women's dresses and hosiery, more cleaning and beauty products, more "personal accessories," and new household appliances like radios and washing machines. Families also spent more money and time on recreation outside the home. Both urban and rural families consumed these goods and services. A 1930 study of bread consumption, for example, found that most families everywhere had shifted to store-bought goods: 66 percent of farm households, 75 percent of village homes, and 90 percent of urban households. These figures meant that most housewives were now traveling by car to a local baker or A&P to buy what they used to make in their own homes.

Use of the car did not lessen women's household work; rather it helped to change it into many consumer duties. Six studies of the uses of time by farm women during the 1920s concluded that increased conveniences did not decrease their workday: instead of making free time for reading or recreation, they generated more work, such as more laundry, more housekeeping, and—although the studies did not list this—more frequent car trips to town to purchase household goods. . . .

If the automobile did not lessen women's work, why did women and their families accept these changes so readily? The automobile originally offered new possibilities for movement. It especially liberated women from the home. The automobile was a *private* vehicle, and that characteristic made it safer and more acceptable than public streetcars or trains. Even the most genteel women began traveling alone; some wealthier women took cross-country trips together unescorted by male relatives. This "freedom," as many women described the experience of driving, was the positive side to the transformation of women's lives. . . .

As the metropolitan market expanded to include commodities formerly produced at home, the necessity for finding them in village and town centers increased. When the farm woman told the USDA inspector that she couldn't go to town in a bathtub, she was describing the changes in her life which made shopping in town part of her work. And when Middle-town women told the Lynds that they would sacrifice food and clothing before they gave up the family car, they knew that giving up the car meant sacrifices in family consumption.

Differing Attitudes Toward the Car

What began as a vehicle to freedom soon became a necessity. Car movement became the basic form of travel in metropoli-tan consumer society. However, there was nothing inevitable about metropolitan spatial organization or people's uses of cars upon that landscape. The car could have remained a conve-nience used for recreation and cross-movement outside areas serviced by railroads and trolleys, while people continued to use mass transit for daily commutation. Car travel could have remained an option offering certain distinct advantages; in-stead it became a prerequisite to survival. Moreover, this de-pendence upon automobiles was not the outcome of a corpo-rate manipulation of consumer needs. Rather, it resulted from the *reconstitution* of transportation needs within the spatial context of metropolitan society—a reorganization of the phys-ical and social environment which the car facilitated but did not require. Within this spatial context, automobile move-ment became the basic form of travel.

The Depression did not loosen the relationship between Americans and their cars. "If the word 'auto' was writ large across Middletown's life in 1925," the Lynds wrote in *Middle-town in Transition* (1937), "this was even more apparent in 1935, despite six years of Depression." People clung so tena-ciously to their cars, the Lynds observed, because car trans-portation had become a "must" close in importance to food, clothing, and shelter. . . .

Yet if automobile ownership and use had become a basic need by the 1930s, the Lynds also found that people experienced that need and valued car ownership in very different ways. The working class saw the automobile as "their great symbol of ad-vancement. . . . Car ownership stands to them for a large share of the 'American dream'; they cling to it as they cling to self-respect." The business class, in contrast, viewed the car as a lux-ury item which "it is more appropriate for well-to-do people to have . . . than for poor people." Indeed, the business class "regard it as a scandal that some people on relief still manage to operate their cars." These different attitudes reflected a structural dynamic in modern capitalist society. For if the mass production of goods had *democratized* consumption by enlarging the potential market for goods like cars and making ownership contingent solely on the ability to pay, it did not *equalize* consumption. A range of social and economic considerations—for example, the proportion of family income which could be spent on a car—shaped people's identities as consumers and their uses of cars. In other words, inequality continued to affect the ability to consume even though the opportunity to consume became more widespread. The [U.S. government's] Hoover Commission [on Recent Social Trends] in 1933 pointed to this inequality and even a growing rigidity in the American social structure. "The increasing fluidity of the metropolitan community seems to tend toward a local leveling of culture," it wrote, "but at the same time it seems to encourage a system of social stratification."

As both the Hoover Commission and the Lynds noted, these variations in consumption were social rather than individual differences. Take, for example, the experience of suburban residence. Although movement to outlying districts involved both middle-class and working-class urban residents, as well as some rural inhabitants, suburbanization was a differentiated movement. Working-class suburbs and rural villages remained centers of work as well as residence, while middle-class suburbs were strictly residential areas. Indeed, this difference was protected through the use of housing covenants and zoning restrictions on land use, as well as through less formal factors such as the need for workers to remain within commuting distance of their scattered workplaces. In concrete terms, the difference was manifested in the kinds and quality of institutions located within the particular suburb: the presence or absence of noisy and sooty factories, the proportion of single-versus multi-family dwellings, the location of a highway next to or even through a working-class community, and even the kinds of schools available for children. These institutions shaped the experience of everyday life in suburbs: the relation between work and leisure, the character of domestic life and the kinds of household goods purchased by a family, the senses of privacy and autonomy one felt in one's life, and the opportunities for and definition of personal achievement. In short, the degree to which suburban and village residents were able to exert over their social environments infused these residents' attitudes toward their cars. . . .

The Farmer's Car Experience

The experience of suburbanites and village residents differed from that of farm families. Suburbanites used cars for work and consumption. For farmers, the car was more strictly a means of consumption. Car use encouraged a new and unique separation between field work and "domestic" family life. Before the car, farm families had to allocate carefully their use of horses; a two to twelve hour trip into town would exhaust the animal which had to be used for field work the following day. The automobile made such allocation unnecessary by providing a separate vehicle for trips into town, and thus relegated the horse to the field (where it was eventually replaced by the gasoline tractor). Cars thus increased farm families' opportunities for leisure. Yet it was this very separation between farm work and family/recreational activity which distinguished farmers from suburbanites who used their cars to commute to work. And this distinction was grounded in a different relation between work and leisure: farmers lived on their farms/workplaces, while suburbanites travelled from their homes to their offices and factories. These differences affected the experience of automobile use: the distance to be travelled, the purposes behind travel, and the experience of the trip itself.

Of course, the significance of this separation varied for farm owners, tenants and sharecroppers. The difference was not necessarily one of car ownership itself. As many tenants as farmers owned cars: for example, 89 percent of the tenants and 93 percent of the farmers in Iowa in 1926 had automobiles. More important than ownership per se was their use of the car. Economic status affected these different households' consumption of ready-made goods, their use of recreational facilities like movie houses, and their participation in social activities like the Grange [a community improvement association], women's clubs, and state fairs. Family activities outside the farm were also affected by the size of the village center and the kinds of services which it offered to the surrounding community. These factors affected farm households' reliance upon and uses of cars, and thus the degree to which they viewed it as another farm machine or as a pleasure vehicle.

Despite these variations, farm owners and tenants all used the automobile to commute from their farms to town. This relation distinguished them from the migrant labor family. A migrant family's car was not only a means of consumption, it was also the necessary basis for the migrant household's survival as a unit. As migrant labor reorganized around automobile movement, it became necessary to use a car to find work and reach that work as a family unit. The automobile thus dominated the lives of migrant families in a unique and deliberate way. As John Steinbeck wrote in *The Grapes of Wrath* (1939), "the highway became their home and movement their form of expression." Reflecting that relationship, Steinbeck had the Joads always feed the car before they fed themselves.

The Car Did Not Bridge the Urban-Rural Gap

In both urban and rural areas, then, automobile use was shaped by social and economic considerations which lay behind class status: control over income level, workplace location, work hours, job tenure, choice of residence, consumption of household goods, and participation in leisure activities. (And it should be noted, although there is not room here to examine the differences, that these considerations were also affected by race, sex, and age.) These differences characterized people's different needs for transportation within metropolitan society. They remained in the forefront of automobile use because the automobile was a private vehicle which people fit into the fabric of their day to day lives. Thus, if the automobile promoted the reorganization of American space, it did not homogenize the experience of automobile ownership and use within that space.

Increased Car Ownership Spurs Highway Construction in the 1950s

Frank Coffey and Joseph Layden

In the following excerpt from their book on the impact of cars in America, authors Frank Coffey and Joseph Layden discuss the nation's highway boom in the years following World War II. As the authors maintain, the federal government had begun laying out major arteries for commercial transportation as early as 1912, but the concerted effort to create a network of interstate superhighways did not come about until the 1950s. At that time America's soldiers had returned from the war to a prosperous economy, industry was strong, and the nation's new middle class took advantage of the host of manufactured goods that the revved-up economy could produce. Chief among the new purchases for most families was an automobile.

With millions of new cars on the road in the postwar years, the government—backed by automotive powerhouses like General Motors (GM)—devised a strategy to increase the length and number of surface roads and highways in America. The Interstate Highway Act of 1956 proposed laying out forty-

■

Frank Coffey and Joseph Layden, *America on Wheels: The First 100 Years: 1896–1996*. Los Angeles: General Publishing Group, 1996. Copyright © 1996 by PBS. Reproduced by permission of the authors.

one thousand miles of cross-country roadway to handle the swelling number of motor vehicles. The administration of President Dwight D. Eisenhower carried the plan to fruition. As Coffey and Layden assert, Eisenhower did not have a choice in the matter. Although the president was in favor of highway expansion, the sheer number of cars owned by Americans necessitated the paving of America. And, as the author's acknowledge, along with the creation of the interstate highways came the development of America's suburbs—vast tracts of housing where the middle class could live outside of the congestion of the city and still travel to their urban jobs via the highway networks.

Frank Coffey is an author who has written on the United Service Organizations (USO), Elvis Presley, the Dallas Cowboys, and other popular culture topics. Joseph Layden has written books on sports culture.

DRIVING IN THE 1950s BECAME A NATIONAL OBsession. But there were problems. The end of World War II and the ensuing rush of affluence unleashed a torrent of new cars onto the nation's streets and highways. Within a few short years, as the automobile population exploded (the number of cars on the road doubled between 1945 and 1955—from 26 million to 52 million), these thoroughfares became thick with traffic. At times, it was almost impossible to drive from one side of town to the other. The traffic jam, in all its maddening glory, was becoming common. And drivers were losing their patience.

Federal highway acts in 1912, 1921, and 1944 had all provided subsidies for highway construction. The initial efforts focused on improvements to rural roads—to facilitate the transportation of farm produce to market. (As the car population grew and traffic became heavier, busier roads and highways were resurfaced—first with gravel, and later with either concrete or macadam.) States, in turn, were required to match federal dollars. In the 1930s, President Roosevelt's New Deal had made road construction a national priority, and by 1940 major highway construction had begun in Pennsylvania, New

York, and, of course, Southern California. In 1946 surfaced road mileage in the United States surpassed non-surfaced road mileage for the first time; twenty years later more than three-quarters of U.S. road mileage would be surfaced.

Paving California

Los Angeles was one of the great World War II boomtowns, with a population that increased by more than 500,000 between 1940 and 1945. A massive influx of workers was prompted by employment opportunities in the mushrooming defense industry. When the war ended, most of these people stayed; and, since Los Angeles was already becoming a suburban sprawl, nearly all of them were obliged to purchase cars.

The six-lane Arroyo Seco Parkway, completed before the United States' involvement in World War II, was the first step in what would eventually become the most extensive urban freeway system in the world. At a cost of $1.4 million per mile, the Arroyo Seco was also one of the most expensive highways ever produced. It was designed to bring more shoppers into downtown Los Angeles, but instead had just the opposite effect: it allowed people to escape the city and, for better or worse, established a pattern of suburban development. By the time the highway opened, land values in nearby Pasadena had increased by 25 percent. The Arroyo Seco was designed to carry 45,000 people a day; within two decades it would be choked with more than 70,000.

And that was merely the beginning. In 1947 the California state legislature authorized construction of a series of expressways between San Francisco and Los Angeles that would ultimately handle more than 40 percent of the state's traffic. California opted for a freeway system in part because it feared a toll system would only exacerbate potential problems associated with traffic jams. Gasoline and vehicle taxes—intended to target the in-state drivers most likely to use the highways—financed a substantial chunk of the project.

"We were coming out of the war, and everybody wanted their wheels," remembers Dave Roper, a retired California highway engineer. "Everybody wanted Southern California. All these veterans who had been through Southern California as part of their Army experience. They all moved from the

Midwest and the East, back to California, the Promised Land." But the key was mobility. If you were going to take advantage of the opportunities that Southern California offered—the recreational opportunities, the business opportunities, all of those things—you had to have mobility. Not only for people, but for goods. And the freeway system was the answer to that."

During World War II, federal highway construction had been all but abandoned as the nation turned its attention and resources to the war effort. By the 1950s, the rest of the country was looking at California as its model. As the suburbanization of America continued, new and improved roads were desperately needed. And wanted. At the time, little consideration was given to mass transit. The automobile would not conform to the world around it; the world would be reshaped to accommodate the automobile.

"By the end of the Twenties, the highway program had been accepted by the general public as essential," says highway engineer Frank Turner. "Everybody was automotive minded. Highways were the way you got there. That was the way you became an individual in the community. So there was great pressure for rapid improvement of the highway system, enlargement of the system, and to improve it to the point that everybody would have a good road wherever he wanted to go. It was considered one of the citizen's rights, so to speak. An American citizen would have the right to go anywhere, anytime, at his own speed in his own vehicle, by his own mode, and that would be by car. But he had to have a road to do that."

Interstate Highways

Automobile manufacturers were not blind to the desires and concerns of their constituency. Fearful that the motorist might begin to view driving as an unpleasant experience, and thus be less inclined to purchase a new car, the Big Three started lobbying for more highway construction. General Motors, as the industry's dominant corporation, assumed a position of leadership.

"GM in the 1950s certainly had a very large role in shaping public policy," says [historian] Harley Shaiken. "GM may have been in the business of building cars, but as a corporation

GM wanted to insure that there would be an infrastructure for those cars to exist in, and an infrastructure that encouraged more and more people to buy cars. And nowhere was this more important than the interstate highway system."

The Interstate Highway Act of 1956 authorized the construction of a nationwide system of toll-free superhighways. Encompassing some 41,000 miles of highway, at an estimated cost of $27 billion (within 10 years the projected cost would be doubled), it was easily the largest public-works project in history. A whopping 90 percent of the funding for this project would come from the federal government, presumably through gasoline and use taxes. . . .

The Eager Industry and the Willing Administration

By the 1950s it was generally accepted that the automobile had become an enormously effective economic tool. If the American consumer wanted to buy a new home in the suburbs, he needed not only a car to get there, but also a road on which to travel. The automobile industry appeared to be nothing less than the key to sustained prosperity. That the paving of America and the eruption of the suburbs would eventually lead to the demise of the American city and prompt isolation and class division on a grand scale was not factored into the equation. At the time, highway expansion meant growth. It meant jobs. It meant money. For the Big Three, it was a multibillion-dollar subsidy.

"The Fifties were a very different climate with the inauguration of Eisenhower as president," says [GM historian] Bradford Snell. "You had an extremely pro-business and pro-automotive administration. When Charles Wilson, formerly president of General Motors, moved in as Secretary of Defense, bringing with him all the General Motors people down to the Pentagon; when other Cabinet posts were filled up and undersecretary positions were filled by General Motors personnel, you in essence had a cabinet that if not favorable towards General Motors, was certainly not resistant to any of their overtures."

Eisenhower established the Clay Commission to write the new highway legislation. That Lucius Clay, who headed the commission, was on the General Motors board of directors barely raised an eyebrow. Nor did it seem to matter that he was working closely with Charles Wilson. No one even suggested the possibility of a conflict of interest.

"Clay was the key person behind drafting Eisenhower and running him as a Republican candidate in the 1952 election," notes Snell. "And at that point, of course, Clay was already in with General Motors and was privy to all the interstate highway system plans. So it was almost inevitable that when Eisenhower was inaugurated and got into office and [GM head Alfred P.] Sloan brought down the plans, that Clay would be named head of the committee to investigate the merits of this measure.

"I believe the Clay committee had just two days of hearings. It was a *fait accompli*. It was something that General Motors wished to have. And Eisenhower was totally in favor of it. It was something that was going to happen."

Highway to the Suburbs

Postwar highway expansion, not coincidentally, was paralleled by the growth of suburbia. The suburban population in the United States increased by nearly 50 percent in the 1950s, changing forever the way Americans lived and worked. Unlike the denizens of the first suburbs, which sprouted shortly after the turn of the century, suburbanites of the 1950s tended not to live along trolley or rail lines, which funneled neatly into city centers. Instead, they took up residence in manufactured communities far from the urban crush.

And they never looked back. . . .

"Suburbia has had a tremendously damaging effect on the civic life of our country," says [historian] James Kunstler. "What suburbia has done is taken all the activities of our lives and dispersed them into separate pods which we are compelled to drive to. So, first of all, it's fantastically expensive to use suburbia on an everyday basis. And it has taken what were once integral neighborhoods and cities, in which the different activities were all interlinked and easy to get to, and it has exploded them and smeared them out over the landscape. And this new suburban landscape that we have created has none of the characteristics of a town or city and none of the characteristics of the country."

The sociopolitical implications of the suburbs were not

really of any great concern to the automobile industry. To Detroit, the suburbs represented a vast new market, and they were embraced as such. The automobile companies began to promote the idea that each family needed a car . . . or two cars. Maybe three. Dad needed a car to drive to work; mom needed a car to chaperone the kids to school or baseball practice, and to do the grocery shopping. And, eventually, as the children became teenagers, with social lives of their own, they too would need wheels. Americans bought into this philosophy, in large part because it was absolutely true. Families in the suburbs really did need more than one car. And by 1960 statistics reflected this fact: nearly one-third of American households owned at least two cars.

Nevertheless, Frank Turner argues, "We didn't create suburbia by putting in a road. It's the other way around. Suburbia came along because people didn't want to live downtown. They could and did move out somewhere else. Virtually all of those suburbs were developed long before there was a road out there. And that's the first bitching that the suburban residents came up with: 'Hey, we can't get to town here. This road's terrible. It's blocked and jammed and everything.' Well, we didn't move them out there. They came to us after the fact and said we need transportation."

Whether the highway gave rise to the suburbs or the suburbs gave rise to the highway is a point of contention. What cannot be debated, however, is that both are by-products of the automobile.

The Car Transforms Family Relationships

James J. Flink

The automobile is an intrinsic part of American life. Almost every household in the country owns at least one automobile, and according to James J. Flink, its impact on the family unit since the 1920s has been significant. In the following article Flink asserts that cars gave family members a new sense of independence. Women, for example, found that the automobile offered them more flexibility and more mobility in the completion of daily chores, and as a result, they had time to be more socially involved. In addition, teens could escape constant parental supervision while behind the wheel of the family car, drastically altering the nature of courtship behavior. The family automobile, in Flink's opinion, also contributed to the reshaping of the neighborhood landscape as independent retailers were driven out of business by one-stop supermarkets, fast-food franchises, and drive-in movie theaters catering to the car culture. Soon the garage replaced the front porch as the main entryway into the home.

James J. Flink is a professor at the University of California at Irvine and one of America's foremost historians of automotive culture. He has written three books on the subject: *The Car Culture; America Adopts the Automobile, 1895–1910;* and *The Automobile Age*, from which this article is taken.

■

BEGINNING IN THE 1920s FOR THE MIDDLE CLASS and in the 1950s for the working class, automobility revolutionized the lifestyle of the typical American family. Despite the development of rudimentary automobile cultures in the advanced capitalist countries of Western Europe and in Japan in the post–World War II period, the family car remains a uniquely American institution; in the words of French sociologist Jean-Jacques Chanaron, "Except for North America, the automobile [still] is not integrated into the banality of daily life."

Family togetherness was a major benefit anticipated by early proponents of automobility. "Next to the church there is no factor in American life that does so much for the morals of the public as does the automobile," E.C. Stokes, a former governor of New Jersey and the president of a Trenton bank, claimed in 1921. "Any device that brings the family together as a unit in their pursuit of pleasure is a promoter of good morals and yields a beneficent influence that makes for the good of American civilization. If every family in the land possessed an automobile, family ties would be closer and many of the problems of social unrest would be happily resolved. . . . The automobile is one of the country's best ministers and best preachers."

Intergenerational Conflict

Contrary to Stokes's widely shared expectations, by the end of the decade it was evident that any tendency of automobility to bring the family together was ephemeral—although an increasing number of people did find the Sunday drive a preferable alternative to attending church. "No one questions the use of the auto for transporting groceries, getting to one's place of work or the golf course, or in place of the porch for 'cooling off after supper,'" [sociologists] Robert and Helen Lynd found in their 1929 study [of families in Muncie, Indiana, which they nicknamed "Middletown"]. "But when auto riding tends to replace the traditional call in the family parlour as a way of approach between the unmarried, 'the home is endangered,' and all-day Sunday motor trips are a 'threat against the church'; it is in the activities concerned with the home and religion that the automobile occasions the greatest emotional conflicts."

Although in theory the family car could bring husbands, wives, and children together in their leisure-time activities, the divorce rate continued to climb in the 1920s, and conflicts between parents and children reached a new height during the decade. A major source of intergenerational conflict in Middletown was the use of the family car. There is no evidence that the motorcar contributed to the divorce rate, but then neither did it, as early proponents of automobility expected, stop the divorce mill from grinding.

That the motorcar undercut parental supervision and authority is unequivocal. "The extensive use of this new tool by the young has enormously extended their mobility and the range of alternatives before them; joining a crowd motoring over to a dance in a town twenty miles away may be a matter of a moment's decision, with no one's permission asked," the Lynds pointed out. "Furthermore, among the high school set, ownership of a car by one's family has become an important criterion of social fitness: a boy almost never takes a girl to a dance except in a car; there are persistent rumors of the buying of a car by local families to help their children's social standing in high school."

In Southern California the automobile had become by the mid-1920s "a social essential" for teenagers: dating now required a car, and "the automobile was seen as a tremendous threat to parental control, enabling children to escape entirely and with great ease from all the restrictions of their home environments." A 1921 report from the captain of the Los Angeles County motorcycle squad to the Board of Supervisors noted "Numerous complaints have been received of night riders who park their automobiles along country boulevards, douse their lights and indulge in orgies." In a 1925 address the Pasadena police chief complained that "the astounding number of 'coupe lovers' who park on dark streets in the Crown City necessitates the use of nearly all the police machines on patrol duty.". . .

Courtship and Mating

The impact of the automobile on courtship and mating has been most thoroughly studied and wittily portrayed by [author] David L. Lewis. "Cars fulfilled a romantic function from the dawn of the auto age," he writes. "They permitted couples to get much farther away from front porch swings, parlor sofas, hovering mothers, and pesky siblings than ever before. . . .

Courtship itself was extended from the five-mile radius of the horse and buggy to ten, twenty, and fifty miles and more. Sociologists duly noted that increased mobility provided by the motorcar would lead to more cross-breeding and eventually improve the American species." However, autos did more than facilitate romantic love among couples who would marry and settle down to rear children. "They also have influenced American culture by abetting prostitution, creating the 'hot pillow' trade in tourist courts and motels, [and] providing an impetus for drive-in restaurants and movies."

The traditional visit on the veranda or parlor call was replaced by the automobile date to a dance or movie that ended up in the local lovers' lane. No one ever has proved that the 38-inch-long seat of a Model T was more convenient or comfortable than a haystack, and Henry Ford allegedly designed the Model T seat so short to discourage the use of his car as a place in which to engage in sexual intercourse. But determined couples found ways to thwart Ford's intentions, and the auto makers came to facilitate lovemaking in cars with such innovations as heaters, air conditioning, and the tilt steering wheel. The 1925 Jewett introduced the fold-down bed, and the bed conversion option on Nash cars after 1937 became popular as "the young man's model." The height of accommodation to sexual drive in automobile design came in the vans of the 1970s, called by Lewis "the most sexually oriented vehicles ever built." Van owners tended to be single men under 35 years of age; and vans featured interiors with all the amenities of a bordello and suggestive exterior murals and slogans that, in Lewis's words, "leave no doubt as to their owner's motives. . . . Vans also are a prostitute's motorized dream."

Thousands of drive-in fast-food stands were built at the edges of towns in the 1920s and 1930s, after the first, Royce Hailey's Pig Stand, was opened in Dallas in 1921, and the Pig Stand Company was formed. The drive-ins served hamburgers and hot dogs washed down with soft drinks or milk shakes, to patrons who remained in their cars. The food was delivered on trays by low-paid teenaged help, called carhops. A&W, which followed the Pig Stand Company into business with its national chain of drive-ins in 1924, introduced "tray girls," who became a major attraction to the main patrons of the drive-ins—youths cruising in cars in search of sexual adventure. In most areas of the country, the drive-in business was seasonal. Many cities passed restrictive legislation to abate the nuisance of drive-in noise and litter. At the height of their popularity in the mid-1960s, there were some 35,000 drive-in eateries in the United States, with California and Texas leading in numbers.

Drive-In Movie Theaters

The first drive-in movie theater was opened in Camden, New Jersey, on June 6, 1933, by Richard M. Hollingshead, Jr., who was granted a patent on the idea. With his cousin, Willis Warren Smith, owner of a chain of parking lots, Hollingshead formed Park-In Theaters, opened a second drive-in theater on Pico Boulevard in Los Angeles in 1934, and began selling his idea to other entrepreneurs for a fee of $1,000 plus 5 percent of their gross receipts. The drive-in theater consisted of a giant screen; a building that housed a projection room, a stand dispensing soft drinks and snacks, and rest rooms; and rows of parking spaces on a large lot on the outskirts of town. Relatively low overhead costs compared with those of downtown theaters were passed on in the form of low admission prices, and family patrons had neither to dress up nor to worry about leaving young children at home with a babysitter. The main drawback was that, like the drive-in food stand, the drive-in theater was a seasonal business closed for the winter months in most areas of the country. . . .

Drive-in theaters made special attempts to appeal to a predominantly family trade, both in the low admissions charged and in the provision of special facilities to amuse children, such as playgrounds and animal parks. Nevertheless, they quickly gained reputations as "passion pits" where the show in the cars was usually better than the one on the screen.

Similarly, the cabin camps that came to dot the roadside after 1925 were assailed by FBI chief J. Edgar Hoover in 1940 as "camouflaged brothels." He claimed that many so-called tourist courts refused accommodations to travelers to concentrate on the more lucrative local "couples trade" and that some Texas cabins were rented as many as sixteen times a night, while others provided prostitutes.

Mobile lovemaking has declined appreciably in the United States since the 1970s. Urban sprawl, a result of auto-induced decentralization, has diminished greatly the availability of safe trysting spots. Gas-guzzling vans have become less popular with escalating oil prices following the oil shocks of 1973 and 1979. The downsizing of passenger cars places severe limits on the possible positions for expressing passion. Most important, changing sexual mores and standards of community and parental acceptance have resulted in living arrangements that make mobile lovemaking largely unnecessary. "Who needs cars when beds are so readily available?" Lewis asks rhetorically.

Changing Woman's Role

Motor Trend in 1967 cited a survey showing that out of 1,100 marriages nearly 40 percent had been proposed in an automobile. Motorization profoundly affected the lifestyles of middle-class couples whose "spoon, moon, and June" back-seat romance rhymed with family life in a suburban home.

To begin with, as early as the 1920s automobility was making the role of the middle-class housewife vastly different from her mother's. Despite the traditional association of the automobile as a mechanical object with men and masculinity in American culture, automobility probably has had a greater impact on women's roles than on men's, and women have been enamored of the motorcar from the outset of its diffusion.

Because driving an automobile requires skill rather than physical strength, women could control one far easier than they could a spirited team [of horses]. They were at first primarily users of electric cars, which were silent, odorless, and free from the problems of hand-cranking to start the engine and shifting gears. Introduction of the self-starter in 1912, called the "ladies' aid," and of the closed car after 1919, which obviated wearing special clothes while motoring, put middle-class women drivers in conventional gasoline automobiles in droves. Most of the comfort and convenience options added to cars since then—including vanity mirrors, plush upholstery, heaters, air conditioning, and automatic transmissions—were innovated with the ladies especially in mind. . . .

Despite a pervasive myth to the contrary, as early as 1925 the American Automobile Association announced that tests had proved conclusively that women drivers were not only as competent as men but even more stable and predictable in their responses to driving situations. Statistics on motor vehicle accidents and traffic violations continue to bear this out and to demonstrate that the most dangerous drivers are young males.

Until the automobile revolution, in upper-middle-class households groceries were either ordered by phone and delivered to the door or picked up by domestic servants or the husband on his way home from work. Iceboxes provided only very limited space for the storage of perishable foods, so shopping at markets within walking distance of the home was a daily chore. The garden provided vegetables and fruits in season, which were home-canned for winter consumption. Bread, cakes, cookies, and pies were home-baked. Wardrobes contained many home-sewn garments. Mother supervised the household help and worked alongside them preparing meals, washing and ironing, and house cleaning. In her spare time she mended clothes, did decorative needlework, puttered in her flower garden, and pampered a brood of children. Generally, she made few family decisions and few forays alone outside the yard. She had little knowledge of family finances and the family budget. The role of the lower-middle-class housewife differed primarily in that far less of the household work was done by hired help, so that she was less a manager of other people's

Women's roles changed dramatically when housewives embraced the freedom the automobile brought into their lives and daily routines.

work, more herself a maid-of-all-work around the house.

Automobility freed such women from the narrow confines of the home and changed them from producers of food and clothing into consumers of national-brand canned goods, prepared foods, and ready-made clothes. The automobile permitted shopping at self-serve supermarkets outside the neighborhood and in combination with the electric refrigerator made buying food a weekly rather than a daily activity. The car also permitted attendance at movie matinees followed by downtown shopping sprees or getting together with the girls for lunch or an afternoon of bridge.

Far less household help was needed, as the household stopped being a producer of many items, and as domestic servants were replaced by a bevy of increasingly sophisticated electric vacuum cleaners, ranges and ovens, mixmasters, irons, washing machines, and clothes dryers. Control of the family budget inevitably passed to Mother as she took over the shopping and became the family expert on the technology of household appliances.

She was the primary user of the family car, for shopping, for carting the kids to school and Little League practice, and for a myriad of other activities. Consequently, her views on what kind of car the family needed often became a mandate for the purchase of a nine-passenger station wagon. "By midcentury," writes [author] Ruth Schwartz Cowan, "the automobile had become, to the American housewife of the middle classes, what the cast-iron stove in the kitchen would have been to her counterpart of 1850—the vehicle through which she did much of her most significant work, and the work locale where she could be most often found."

Domestic Economy

Folklore notwithstanding, the impact of the automobile on the bedroom has been far less profound than its impact on the kitchen. And it was the kitchen that was the heart of the turn-of-the-century middle-class home.

In conjunction with electric kitchen appliances, particularly the refrigerator, the automobile transformed shopping and food preparation. The electric refrigerator with freezing compartment, which permitted large amounts of perishable foods to be purchased at one time and stored until needed, was appropriately developed and popularized by GM's Frigidaire Division and by Nash-Kelvinator during the 1920s and 1930s. Now it was possible to load up the car with a week's worth of food—more and more of it partially prepared convenience food—at a one-stop, self-serve market whose prices were lower than those at the specialty stores.

Prior to the widespread diffusion of the automobile-refrigerator complex, shopping for foodstuffs and housewares was virtually an everyday chore, at a series of retail specialty stores operated by the dry goods merchant, the butcher, the fishmonger, the produce dealer, and the baker. Orders read to clerks were boxed from stocked shelves behind a counter in the grocery store. Meats were cut to order and wrapped by the butcher. Fresh vegetables were selected under the peddler's watchful eye. Credit was extended to steady customers, and phoned-in orders were delivered to the door. The large amount of store labor necessitated by this personal service, together with uneconomical wholesale purchasing in small lots, resulted in relatively high retail prices for foodstuffs.

The self-service market was introduced by Clarence Saunders, who opened his first Piggly Wiggly store in Memphis, Tennessee, in 1916 and patented the idea. Instead of reading orders to a clerk behind a counter, the customer entered the Piggly Wiggly through a turnstile, picked up a basket, and followed a one-way "circuitous path" along which groceries were stacked, including perishables in refrigerated cases. The path ended at a "settlement and checking department," where the prices of the goods selected by the customer were totaled on an adding machine and the purchases were bagged by a checker. The innovation won immediate popularity, and the changeover of retail food sales to self-service was evident by the early 1920s. By the end of that decade over 2,600 Piggly Wigglys were in operation.

Simultaneously, there was a movement away from independently owned small specialty stores to chain stores that could purchase in large lots and pass the savings on to customers, and to "combination stores" that sold a full range of foodstuffs under the same roof. The largest corporate chain was the Atlantic and Pacific Tea Company (A&P). Founded on the eve of the Civil War, the A&P mushroomed from only 372 stores in 1920 to over 16,000 by 1927, compared to some 4,000 stores for Kroger, A&P's chief corporate-chain rival. . . .

The kitchen began to lose its status as the center of household activity as shopping and food preparation came to require far less time, and moreover as automobility encouraged families to eat out far more often. Automobile tourism created a demand for wayside family restaurants, and a meal out became the capstone of the Sunday drive or weekend automobile outing for hungry, tired families. [Highway historian] Chester H. Liebs points out that coincident with the rise of mass personal automobility, "the nation . . . entered a full-fledged eating-out boom, with the estimated number of restaurants jumping 40 percent between 1910 and 1927." The experience of eating out also changed dramatically for the middle-class family—from a leisurely, full-course meal in the formal atmosphere of a hotel dining room, to the quick pickup of a hamburger and french fries in a come-as-you-are roadside diner. . . .

Hearth and Home

Automobility transformed the architecture of the American middle-class house. [Architectural historian] Folke T. Kihlstedt describes this process of change, beginning with the pre-automobile era, when "the front porch still functioned as the buffer zone between the privacy of the house and the communality of the neighborhood. . . . The parlor and the front porch supported a formal style of life . . . built around an accepted social hierarchy in which a progression of architectural spaces, from front porch (or veranda) to hall to parlor to library (or sitting room) and to dining room, were related to increasing degrees of intimacy." The unsightliness and stench of the stable kept it located away from the house at the back of a large lot.

By removing leisure-time activities away from the home and the neighborhood, automobility, [says Kihlstedt] "offset the need for a large house with many rooms into which one could escape and seek privacy." The front porch and the parlor were eliminated as the home became more of a dormitory and rooms lost their former specialized functions. Fear of the danger of gasoline storage, enforced by building codes, zoning laws, and higher insurance rates, generally kept garages detached from houses until after World War II. But under the leadership of Frank Lloyd Wright, architects were designing houses with integrated garages for middle-class clients by the mid-1930s. Wright's 1930s "usonian" houses developed the carport and made it necessary to walk down the driveway and under the carport to find the front door. "In contrast to a turn-of-the-century house, the house of 1945 has no hall, no parlor, and a mere vestige of a porch," Kihlstedt observes. "The garage was moved from the back of the lot to the front of the suburban house, and adjacent to the front door. . . . Entry is directly into the living and dining rooms, or into the kitchen through the adjoining garage. The element that projects far-thest toward the street to greet the passer-by is no longer a shaded and generous porch. It is the large prominent surface of the garage door."

This prominence of the driveway and direct entry into the kitchen from the garage turned the suburban home into an ex-tension of the street. So much so that sidewalks were elimi-nated from many post–World War II housing tracts. The blending of the house into the highway has proceeded furthest in auto-dominated Southern California. "A domestic or socia-ble journey in Los Angeles," notes [L.A. historian] Reyner Banham, "does not so much end at the door of one's destina-tion as at the off-ramp of the freeway, the mile or two of ground-level streets counts as no more than the front drive of the house.". . .

Community: From Neighbor to Night Dweller

The new mobility of families was destroying the traditional pat-tern of close relationships among neighbors by the 1920s. Wrote the Lynds, "The housewife with leisure does not sit so much on the front porch afternoons after she 'gets dressed up,' sewing and 'visiting' and comparing her yard with her neigh-bors', nor do the family and neighbors spend long summer evenings and Sunday afternoons on the porch or in the side yard since the advent of the automobile and the movies." Automo-bility had made "a decorative yard less urgent." "In the [eigh-teen] nineties we were all much more together," a Middletown housewife explained. "People brought chairs and cushions out of the house and sat on the lawns evenings. We rolled out a strip of carpet and put cushions on the porch step to take care of the unlimited overflow of neighbors that dropped by. . . . The younger couples perhaps would wander off for half an hour to get a soda but come back to join in the informal singing or listen while somebody strummed a mandolin or guitar."

Such a scene contrasts sharply with the conception of neighborliness revealed by a 1929 survey [conducted by Bessie Averne McClenahan of the University of Southern California] of the residents of a twenty-block middle-class section of Los Angeles near the USC campus. . . . [She] found that "a new definition of a friendly neighborhood is apparent; it is one in which the neighbors tend to their own business." One householder explained: "We have nothing whatsoever to do with my neighbors. I don't even know their names or know them to speak to. My best friends live in the city but by no means in this neighborhood. We belong to no clubs and we do not attend any local church. We go auto riding, visiting and uptown to the theaters.". . . [McClenahan] concluded, "This straining against the bonds that hold them in the area makes for many families an uneasy, unsettled, uncertain state." But another observer of 1920s Los Angeles [Emery S. Bogardus] interpreted the phenomenon positively: "The role particularly of the automobile . . . has cut down spatial distance and tended to increase social nearness to such an extent that every person may live in wide-flung communalities of his own [making], in place of the old closely circumscribed neighborhoods."

Road Rage: The Unsubstantiated Epidemic

Michael Fumento

While traveling the alluring roads of America, drivers
are constantly faced with the grim reality of highway
dangers—whether from an unforeseen mechanical
failure or a terrible accident. In the late 1990s a
new form of traffic-related anxiety hit the national
agenda: road rage. Since the coining of the term in
1988, experts have rarely agreed on a definition of
road rage, but it is most often characterized as a form
of aggressive driving. This loose description, though,
has made the term applicable to everything from a
passing motorist's offensive gestures to roadside
homicide. Throughout the 1990s the expression became prevalent in news stories and headlines in which
highway accidents and fatalities were blamed on the
acts of irate and sometimes vindictive drivers. According to Michael Fumento, the author of the following article, Congress was even prompted in 1996
to treat road rage seriously by ordering a study of this
seemingly new and deadly highway mentality.

    Fumento contends, however, that while the media
have blown this social malady up to epidemic proportions, the reality of road rage is not supported by the
statistics. The number of highway fatalities and accidents, Fumento maintains, is either holding steady or,
in some cases, is declining in proportion to the escalated number of drivers on the road. Furthermore, Fu-

■

THE CAR'S IMPACT ON SOCIETY

mento argues that the term *road rage* is nothing more than a fancy label, popularized by journalists and lobbyists to sensationalize behavior that has been part of America's driving experience since the dawn of the auto age. Fumento claims that even if motorists are becoming more aggressive, road rage poses no real increased danger on the nation's highways. He therefore calls upon interest groups to redirect their focus to more tangible roadway threats. Fumento is a syndicated columnist, science and health lecturer, and attorney.

"ROAD WARRIORS: AGGRESSIVE DRIVERS TURN FREEWAYS INTO FREE-FOR-ALLS," read the headline of an Associated Press article in the *Chicago Tribune* last year [1997]. "Armed with everything from firearms to Perrier bottles to pepper spray and eggs," the text began. "America's drivers are taking frustrations out on each other in startling numbers.". . . In January of [1998] *Time* declared, "It's high noon on the country's streets and highways. This is road recklessness, auto anarchy, an epidemic of wanton carmanship.". . .

The media couldn't talk enough about the awful carnage. . . . By July of last year matters had become so serious that Representative Tom Petri, of Wisconsin, called hearings before the House Subcommittee on Surface Transportation, which he chairs. "It's a national disaster," Jeff Nelligan, a committee staff member, said. "It's making our roads some of the most dangerous places in the country."

By the end of May [1997] there were about 200 citations on the Nexis media database that used both "epidemic" and "road rage." In fact, there's been a tremendous proliferation of the term "road rage" itself. It was apparently coined in 1988, and appeared in up to three stories yearly until 1994, when it began to catch on. After twenty-seven mentions that year the numbers escalated sharply, to almost 500 in 1995, more than 1,800 in 1996, and more than 4,000 in 1997.

Headlines notwithstanding, there was not—there is not—the least statistical or other scientific evidence of more-aggressive driving on our nation's roads. Indeed, accident, fatality, and injury rates have been edging down. There is no evidence that "road rage" or an aggressive-driving "epidemic" is anything but a media invention, inspired primarily by something as simple as a powerful alliteration: road rage. The term was presumably based on "roid rage," referring to sudden violent activity by people on steroids. The term, and the alleged epidemic, were quickly popularized by lobbying groups, politicians, opportunistic therapists, publicity-seeking safety agencies, and the U.S. Department of Transportation.

AAA's Numbers

The most frequently cited evidence that Americana have been killing and maiming one another at record rates was a study from the American Automobile Association [AAA] Foundation for Traffic Safety, released in March of [1997]. . . . The study,

"Instructive" Driving Behavior

In the following extract Jason Vest, Warren Cohen, and Mike Tharp discuss the possible causes of road rage, including increased traffic congestion and more time spent behind the wheel.

Unfortunately, *roads* are getting more congested just as Americans feel even more pressed for time. "People get on a time line for their car trips," says [professor in the health education and safety department at Minnesota's St. Cloud State University, John] Palmer. "When they perceive that someone is impeding their progress or invading their agenda, they respond with what they consider to be 'instructive' behavior, which might be as simple as flashing their lights to something more combative.". . .

This, . . . "instruction" has become more common, Palmer and others speculate, in part because of modern automotive design. With hyperadjustable seats, soundproof interiors, CD players, and cellular phones, cars are virtually comfortable enough to live in. Students of traffic can't help but wonder if the popularity of pickup trucks and sport utility vehicles has contributed to the problem [of road rage].

however, was quite possibly a measure more of perception than of reality.

To conduct it, AAA commissioned Mizell & Co., of Bethesda, Maryland, a consulting firm that collects criminal statistics. The study purported to show an increase of about 60 percent in what it termed "aggressive driving" from 1990 through 1996 (if the rate applicable partway through 1996 held constant). . . .

The study has numerous problems. Consider that the 218 deaths Mizell claimed were directly attributable to aggressive driving occurred in a period during which 290,000 people died in traffic accidents. He identified 12,610 people whose injuries were attributable to aggressive driving out of a total of 23 million people injured by vehicles. And the survey was hardly sci-

Sales have approximately doubled since 1990. These big metal shells loom over everything else, fueling feelings of power and drawing out a driver's more primal instincts. "A lot of the anecdotal evidence about aggressive driving incidents tends to involve people driving sport utility vehicles," says Julie Rochman of the Insurance Institute for Highway Safety. "When people get these larger, heavier vehicles, they feel more invulnerable." While Chrysler spokesman Chris Preuss discounts the notion of suburban assault vehicles being behind the aggressive-driving phenomenon, he does say women feel more secure in the jumbo-size vehicles.

In much of life, people feel they don't have full control of their destiny. But a car—unlike, say, a career or a spouse —responds reliably to one's wish. In automobiles, we have an increased (but false) sense of invincibility. Other drivers become dehumanized, mere appendages to a competing machine. "You have the illusion you're alone and master, dislocated from other drivers," says [University of Hawaii traffic psychology professor Sean James].

Jason Vest, Warren Cohen, and Mike Tharp, "Road Rage," *U.S. News & World Report*, June 1997.

entific. Rather, Mizell simply drew on stories from about thirty newspapers, reports from sixteen police departments, and insurance-company claim reports. He didn't even demonstrate that the changes in his numbers from year to year were statistically significant. Couldn't an increase in the number of incidents reported simply reflect increased awareness of and publicity for aggressive driving, along with an explosion in the use of the term "road rage"?

Labeling an Unexplained Phenomenon

David Murray, the director of research at the Statistical Assessment Service, in Washington, D.C., doesn't buy it. Once a phenomenon picks up a label, he explains, the label tends to be applied to more and more things. "We find it everywhere," Murray says. "There has always been a degree of aggression while driving, but what did we used to call it? Nothing. Now that we have a name, we look for things that seem to be similar and build a pathology.". . .

An employee in the Traffic Safety Program at the National Highway Traffic Safety Administration [NHTSA], whose comments have to go without attribution because the NHTSA press office wouldn't let her speak on the record . . . candidly admitted that although aggressive driving is "a newly emerging issue," "no data" indicate an actual increase in it. "Not here and not anywhere," she emphasized. "Aggressive driving" is "just a term," she explained, with "no fixed definition." "There's no law against anything called 'aggressive driving,' and therefore no tally to look at, as with speeding tickets," she said. "You have to have something to mark."

Inconclusive Fatality Statistics

If road rage were increasingly a problem, shouldn't it show up in an increase in highway fatalities? Political appointees at the NHTSA—as opposed to those who actually collect and analyze the data—claim that it does. Ricardo Martinez, the head of the NHTSA, told Petri's subcommittee. "After years of steady decline, the total number of highway deaths increased slightly in each of the last four years." He added that in 1996 there were 41,907 highway fatalities in the country, an increase from the year before.

But those numbers don't take into account additional drivers or miles driven. During the period in which the AAA survey found a 60 percent increase in aggressive-driving accidents, deaths on American highways actually declined, to 1.7 per 100 million vehicle miles traveled. In 1987, the year before "road rage" first appeared on Nexis, the rate was 2.4. . . .

As for injuries, in 1990, the first year of the Mizell data, there were 151 per 100 million miles traveled. By 1996 the number had slipped to 141. Preliminary NHTSA data for 1997 show that motor-vehicle deaths, crashes, and injuries all declined in absolute terms, despite an increase in vehicle miles traveled of about two percent.

None of this is proof that no increase has occurred in the number of deaths or injuries attributable to road rage. After all, improvements in auto safety may have more than compensated for increases in road-rage casualties. But it's clear that authorities are being disingenuous when they claim that casualty data are worsening.

Road Rage Too Broadly Defined

Still, aggressive driving does cause some accidents. At Petri's subcommittee hearings Martinez claimed that "one third of these crashes and about two thirds of the resulting fatalities can be attributed to behavior associated with aggressive driving." The media accepted this claim without question: "TEMPER CITED AS CAUSE OF 28,000 ROAD DEATHS A YEAR" (*The New York Times*). . . . But was there any truth to the figure of 28,000? Liz Neblett, a spokeswoman for the NHTSA, responded quite candidly. "We don't have hard numbers," she said, "but aggressive driving is almost everything. It includes weaving in and out of traffic, driving too closely, flashing your lights—all kinds of stuff. Drinking, speeding, almost everything you can think of, can be boiled down to aggressive driving behaviors." With such a broad definition, Martinez could conceivably label virtually every accident as the result of aggressive driving.

Originally "road rage" meant one driver acting against another. No longer. By last year it had come to include a Washington, D.C., bicyclist who shot the driver of a car who ran into him, and a Scottish couple who threatened a driver with a knife after his BMW ran over their dog. The definition of "road rage" now requires neither a road nor rage. One newspaper published a story about developing pristine land under the headline "ROAD RAGE HAS TAKEN TOLL ON WILDERNESS," and *USA Today* discussed people angry about their insurance premiums under the headline "DRIVERS FEEL 'ROAD RAGE' OVER HIGH INSURANCE RATES."

Driving behavior that was once called something else is now called road rage. Thus a British insurance firm recently conducted a poll in which, it claims, "almost one in two state they have either been a victim of or a witness to an act of 'Road Rage.'" But the primary road-rage act was "verbal abuse," the second largest category was "hand gestures," and the third was "intimidatory driving." Attacks on vehicles or people were rarely reported. . . .

Treat the Disease, Not the Symptoms

While roads become slightly safer each year, traffic accidents remain a leading cause of death in this country, and disproportionately so among the young. But the fuss over aggressive driving and road rage distracts us from those behaviors that could be controlled with relatively minor investments, greatly reducing deaths and injuries. . . .

Clearly a major factor in American road deaths and injuries is that it is ridiculously easy in this country to get a driver's license—to drive a couple of tons of metal capable of going more than 100 miles per hour. . . .

How many more lives could be saved and injuries prevented if we focused on behaviors that cause accidents, rather than on media creations like road rage?

2

EXAMINING POP CULTURE

Car Cultures

Hot-Rodders and Customizers

Paul Rambali

In the following selection author Paul Rambali examines hot-rodders and car customizers, two groups of
automobile enthusiasts that sprang up in the United
States during the 1950s. According to Rambali, both
of these groups were obsessed with the potential
speed of automobiles—the hot-rodders retooled their
vehicles to increase velocity, while the customizers
"restyled" their cars to at least give the illusion of
speed. As Rambali notes, the majority of these enthusiasts were teenagers and young adults from the West
Coast, and they often banded together in local car associations. Members of hot-rod clubs tested their
bravado in arena speed trials or in street races. Customizers displayed their extravagantly painted and reshaped cars at car shows or at the local hangout. By
the 1960s the popularity of these subcultures compelled major car manufacturers to cash in on the
craze by offering commercial automobiles with more
powerful engines and custom add-ons. It did not take
long before these fads made their way into the mainstream. Paul Rambali wrote the text that accompanies
the photo layouts in the pictorial history *Car Culture*.

IT'S A MISAPPREHENSION TO THINK OF THE HOT-
rodder as the owner of a 1930s stripped-down, highboy roadster, prone to anti-social behaviour and destined to cool his
heels in reform school if not, after the inevitable high-speed

■

spill, in the local morgue. The owner of the stripped-down highboy might equally be a customiser, not especially concerned about the power of the engine, but determined that the thing should look 'neat'.

Faced with the Chrysler Saratoga—and money being no object—he would chop the roof height by three or four inches, lower or 'channel' the body down over the wheels by about the same amount, and maybe alter the shape of the fenders at the same time, replace the door handles with hidden electric solenoids, remove all the trim and weld over the holes, 'french' the headlights and aerial, and lastly swap the bumpers, tail lights, hubcaps and grille for those of another car. After several deep, lustrous coats of trick paint had been applied, another radical custom would take, one imagines very gingerly, to the stunned and disconcerted roads.

In some respects, the hot-rodder and the customiser shared the same inspiration: speed was the quest of the hot-rodder, and its look the concern of most customisers. 'My primary purpose for twenty-eight years,' said Harley Earl in a *Saturday Evening Post* article of 1954, 'has been to lengthen and lower the American automobile, at times in reality and always at least in appearance'. The customiser inherited this ideal. Longer and lower was synonymous with faster and sleeker, as Earl well knew; the suggestion, or the look, of speed is often enough.

If it wasn't a crazy car or an extravagant charabanc [a large, open, buslike automobile] that the customiser was after, it was a car that looked faster. All of the more credible (as opposed to incredible) post-war customs sport features that can be traced to the race track; be it removing all the chrome and the fenders, louvring the bonnet [hood], jacking the rear, adding fat tyres or, more recently, adding air foils and front spoilers. The net effect is to invoke speed by way of sympathetic magic. None of these alterations would make a car go very much faster—not without a long programme of testing and adjustment—but they are the paraphernalia of the fast car.

Fast cars, in Europe, are primarily the sport of the rich. In America, after the war, the sport was open to any hot-headed youth who wanted to participate, and participation could occur almost anywhere. Partly money, and partly tradition, made this so. Aside from those in Mexico, there were no established road races of the European sort, and since the collapse of the Cord-Duesenberg-Auburn company in 1935, there had been no US sports car makers of the likes of Lotus or Ferrari for whom a racing commitment was an essential part of their business. In fact, until the Chevrolet Corvette arrived in 1953, followed by the Ford Thunderbird in 1954, there were no US production sports cars.

Speed Arenas

Recognised races in America were confined to the big oval circuit contests like the Indianapolis and Daytona 500s (over a distance of 500 miles) and to the many stocker tracks on which anything that could pass for a production car—the engines were often discreetly modified and always tuned up—could join in a madcap, careening, ricocheting eliminator.

American racing was largely an amateur affair. Industry involvement even in the prestigious 500s was scarce until the 1950s. So-called 'dirt-cars', racing cars scratch-built by either a small team or a lone competitor, were frequent winners at Indianapolis, the last being Troy Ruttman's Agajanian Special in 1952, which set a new track record average of 138.9 mph. The official US racing colours were jokingly held to be grey primer.

Perhaps the greatest arena of speed in America, was the speed trial on the flat. The country's natural geography, and not a few of its roads, offered the perfect opportunity for speed in a straight line—a race against the clock and the limits of mechanical tolerance. Since the turn of the century, places like Daytona beach in Florida, the Bonneville salt flats in Utah, and the California dry lakes had played host to small teams of engineers wheeling strange curvilinear monsters into position and gazing across the flat, shimmering horizon at the unknown edge of landbound motion. Even Europeans who wanted a try were obliged to travel to these venues.

As befits American tradition, the stocker circuits and the speed trials, and even many of the 500s, were frontiers open to individuals and entrepreneurs. One such was Bill Kenz who, in partnership with Roy Leslie, created a hot-rod legend that spanned fifty years, from the occasional backroads duel in the 1920s to the huge commercial circus of drag racing in the 1970s.

The Inspiring Streamliner

Kenz and Leslie's celebrated twin-engined '777' streamliner left a ferocious trail across the hot-rod heyday, winning the *Hot Rod* magazine trophy for top speed five times between 1950 and '57. No doubt teenage hot-rodders of the time would have earned themselves an even worse reputation for public nuisance had they been able to figure out for themselves how to link the crankshafts of two flathead V8s. . . .

In 1949, Kenz and Leslie got word on the growing hot-rod grapevine that a big speed trial was to be held at the Bonneville salt flats. *Hot Rod* magazine had started in 1948 and timing associations were being formed, patterned on the Southern California Timing Association (SCTA), to organise, supervise and quantify the backroad (and sometimes main road) sport of drag racing. Kenz and Leslie reasoned that they would have the drop on the dry lakes racers in that their engines were tuned for the higher altitudes of the Bonneville flats. The [streamliner] pick-up ran up to 141 mph, but more importantly, it introduced the pair to hundreds of hot-rodders from California who shared the same obsessions; a loose fraternity of backyard and workshop motorheads whose country had marshalled all the power of technology to win a war and who were now going to harness part of this power to contraptions that would slake their demon thirst for speed.

The Kenz and Leslie 777 streamliner arrived at Bonneville the following year. It was powered by two 200-hp Edelbrock-equipped flathead Fords and draped in a body of elemental aerodynamic proportions modelled on the So-Cal Special built by Alex Xydias and Dean Batchelor and powered by a single Edelbrock-built Ford Mercury engine that had been the fastest car at the flats in 1949. After some hasty alterations to the air intakes when it was found that the air was flowing so smoothly over the body that not enough of it was entering the carbs, the 777 surpassed its disappointing early speed of 168 mph and reached over 200 mph. 'Everybody on the salt was excited,' recalls [car enthusiast and author] Jay Storer. 'An American home-built hot-rod had exceeded the magic figure of 200 mph and might even go faster.' Eventually the car hit 210 mph, at which speed the treads suddenly ripped from the tyres. Its racing tyres were only good for speeds of up to 175 mph. Luckily, driver Willy Young was able to hold the car to a straight course. When the crew reached him, he wasn't too badly shaken, unlike his watch, which had rattled to pieces.

Hot Rods Take Off in California

'Nobody invented hot-rodding,' said Wally Parks in 1962. 'It just happened.'

Parks was a founder member of the National Hot-Rod Association [NHRA], formed in 1951 as an off-shoot of the SCTA. Throughout the US, but most of all in Southern California, there were people like Bill Kenz, giving cars a performance overhaul, making new parts and modifying old ones. Midwestern and eastern hop-up artists put their work on the track, but in the west they put theirs on the streets, where everyone could see and copy.

The weather was good in California, there was plenty of space to test the cars, and vehicle regulations were not so heavily enforced. So long as a car was not doing anything illegal, the lack of fenders was usually ignored. So, too, was the nose-down racing car look achieved by running Firestone 5 × 16 dirt or sprint car front tyres and slightly larger 7 × 16 rear ones. The car might be built for show or to go, but it was impossible to tell without looking under the bonnet, where, in virtually all of the rods except the real hot cars and nearly half of the customs, there would be a Ford V8, with or without the performance extras.

The perfect post-war rod was a late 1920s early 1930s ragtop roadster. The '32 Ford was the best. It needed no serious body alterations to achieve the ideal line, just a custom dash with Stewart Warner instrument to go with the custom upholstery and paint, removal of all trim right down to the door handles, hydraulic brakes from a later Ford, tail lights from either a '38 Ford or a '41 Chevy, Arrow Accessory sealed-beam headlights, some twin pipes running from a Belond, Douglass or Clark manifold, and perhaps a column gear shift to go with a Zephyr transmission that would squeeze a little more power from first and second.

Once this had 'just happened', in Wally Parks' phrase, who could tell what else might follow? By the mid 1950s, hot-rodders had acquired a notoriety second only to motorcycle gangs. They might descend at any time on a quiet Southern California township, racing their drunken, hopped-up jalopies up and down Main Street, leaving delinquent tyre tracks across respectable driveways, and causing young girls to forget their upbringing.

Movies Follow the Craze

Naturally, this nightmare of society over-run by crazed hot-rodders made very good box office. Vicarious interest ran high in the twilight hoodlum world of loud cars and loose girls, and films with titles like *Hot Rod Girl*, *Dragstrip Girl* and *Hot Rods to Hell* were rushed into production.

Hot Rod Rumble in 1957 was a classic of its kind. 'The scene is a party somewhere in teenland,' wrote Richard Staehling in a survey of teenage B-movies of the 1950s. 'Big Amy is uncouth and dresses flashy. His chick tells him to clean up, and he tells her to forget it. She does just that, riding home with another club member. On the way, a car that looks suspiciously like Big Amy's drives them off the road. Did Amy do it? If not, who did? Only on the day of the "big race" is the mystery solved . . . complete with actual footage of the Pomona drag strip.' If that wasn't delinquent enough, how about *Hot Car Girl* in 1958: 'It's good girls gone bad again, as four teens steal cars, selling them back to a junkyard dealer to make money. When one of the girls kills a motorcycle cop during a chicken race, the trouble really begins.'

Something of a vintage year, 1958 also produced *Dragstrip Riot*, described by its makers as 'the story of teenage youths who live as fast as their hot-rods will carry them'. After a minimal piece of plotting to get things moving (involving, opportunely, a motorcycle gang) we find that 'courage is measured in drag races, the climax building to a free-for-all between the two rival gangs'. All this is liberally salted with 'rock 'n' roll numbers and actual flat races at Santa Barbara, California'. The only things the makers seem to have overlooked are drugs, girls and violent crime. Perhaps it was felt that the popular addition of 'real race footage' would compensate.

Speed Meets

It was probably all far from the truth. On December 12th, 1958, the *LA Times* reported that police had broken up an 'impromptu speed meet' the previous night involving over 100 hot cars on the paved bed of the Los Angeles river. Most of those fined for breaking a by-law against driving on the dry riverbed were teenagers, accompanied by their wives and girl-friends. 'We can't race our cars on the streets,' said one, 'so we come here where we won't be in anyone's way. The drag strips are closed during the week. The police should supervise this deal and let us race here.' It would seem that the fellow was a model hot-rodder. 'We scarcely had time to warm up,' he complained morosely.

More in keeping with the fears of middle America was the riot that occurred in San Diego in 1960 when police used tear gas to disperse a mob of 3,000 that had gathered to watch some street races on an uptown thoroughfare. The crowd had con-

Cruisin'

For hot-rodders and car customizers, restyling automobiles is an expression of male machismo. While they may love the car and its capabilities, both groups toy with flash and speed to get noticed—sometimes at speed trials but more often on main-street thorough-fares where they hope male peers will quake with envy as women stare agog at the revved-up symbols of virility. As writer and cultural historian Michael Karl Witzel emphasizes in this excerpt from Cruisin': Car Culture in America, *hot-rodders and car customizers have always cruised down their hometown's main drag with only one goal—to meet members of the opposite sex.*

Main Street was one big singles bar, and naturally the male of the species flocked there in great numbers. With their hopes inflated by excess hormones, teenage boys who were old enough to pilot two tons of glass and sheet metal—but still too immature to figure out what a woman really wanted in a man—prowled the streets of this two-lane social club with the sole intent of "getting lucky." On a typical Satur-day night in America, most of the young bucks who lacked dates but had cars were trying almost every trick in the cruising book to win over girls and get them to hop into

gregated by word-of-mouth to protest at the closure of a local drag strip. Calls for city sponsorship of a strip as a result of the incident moved Mayor Charles Dail to retort: 'I've never felt it necessary to show kids how fast an automobile will go.'

Nor, by then, was there any need to. They had found out for themselves. The hot-rod had become an amorphous creation, no longer purely a hopped-up Ford roadster. Engines like the big-block Chevy, the Chrysler Hemi and the Cadillac and Oldsmobile V8s were being dropped into any available body and 'blown' by the addition of ram-chargers and outsize headers. It was no longer necessary to bore and measure and modify for speed; bolt-on equipment could be bought over the counter. It was not uncommon to wake from a hellish din the

their chariots. And during the revved-up heyday of cruising, they put on quite a show.

Making a racket gained favor as an effective technique for the cruisers who wanted to call attention to themselves. While one waited at the stoplight, cranking up the radio volume was almost an instinctive reaction—especially if girls pulled up in the other lane. When rock and roll anthems like Elvis' *Heartbreak Hotel* or Jerry Lee Lewis' *Great Balls of Fire* seared the airwaves, there was no controlling the volume level. Revving up the Cherry Bombs (a glass-pack muffler) to make the statement, "Look at me, I'm here, I'm cool, and I'm really loud" was another standard practice. "We used to speed up at the big hill right before Main. As we came over the hump, we let up on the gas pedal to get the mufflers a rumblin'," mused Clark "Crewcut" Taylor, now the operator of a small exhaust repair shop in the West. "These days, making muffler noise is a long forgotten art. Nowadays, it's the loud, rap music and those amplified stereo radio systems with those subwoofer things and all that get the looks!"

Michael Karl Witzel and Kent Bash, *Cruisin': Car Culture in America*. Osceola, WI: Motorbooks, 1997, pp. 49–50.

previous night and find the words 'start' and 'finish' painted on the road outside. By 1965, Los Angeles Police Department citations for 'speed contests' were running at a rate of over 2,000 a year—this can only have been a small percentage of the actual number of infractions.

The hot-rod mecca of the time was Bob's drive-in on Van Nuys Boulevard. On a Friday night cars would queue along several blocks for an empty slot, surrounded by the inevitable crowds of onlookers. Inside, the lore, the legends, and the times and places of street races, would be told by jaws chomping on Big Boy hamburgers. . . .

To Stretch, thirty-two-year-old owner of a modified '62 Corvette and president of the informal Western Avenue Street Racing Association, the street race was a way of life. To the numerous drive-in hot-rod teenagers of the era, it was simply the prevailing method of youthful outburst. Rob Ross quotes a policeman watching the traffic at Bob's: 'There's just not much we can do about it. If two cars pull even at a light, and somebody challenges somebody . . . The problem is that these kids have never seen death. They don't know that their lives can be snuffed out just like *that.*'

The Drag Strip

Wally Parks had shown them speed, and more speed, in the surprisingly safe (compared to Grand Prix or the street) confines of the drag strip. The first NHRA-organised drag races took place in 1948 on a disused strip of the Goleta airfield near Santa Barbara. A quarter-mile from the start there was a hump in the strip, and the winner was whoever hit the hump first. The following year, when the races moved, with official blessing, to the Orange County airfield, the quarter-mile became standard. Other distances were tried but the lengths of these old runways determined the optimum racing distance. Later on, there would be other refinements to the contests: up to sixty classes of competition allowing almost anyone to join in, and the test of 'terminal speed', a top speed measured through 132 feet across the finish (66 ft each side) that allowed, at times, for both cars to win.

'In the early days we used rolling starts,' Wally Parks recalled. 'But it was rare for both cars to hit the starting line together. The next advancement was the standing start. It proved popular, but it also proved expensive to many car owners. The sudden acceleration created a rash of broken rear axles, drive shafts and transmissions'.

This precipitated the era of specialised drag racing vehicles. The more dedicated drivers began to rebuild their roadsters, coupés and saloons with larger, heavy-duty rear axles, adding at the back fat treadless racing 'slicks' for extra traction. In due course this developed into the classic dragster configuration: a long, low lightweight front trailing back to the engine mounted right in front of the rear axle so as to do away with the drive shaft, and the driver sitting just ahead of the engine.

By this time, pro-fuel had become common and drag racing had come a long way from the streets. 'The "Bean Bandits", a group of about twenty Mexican boys from the San Diego area, began to experiment with fuel mixtures,' says Parks. 'They were winning everything in sight until the opposition learned their tricks. Those were the beginnings of fuel dragsters.'

Drag racing started as a healthy participatory event—loose speed meets at which winning was secondary to the swell and the noise and the thrashing of the cars. A traffic-light type of starting signal recalled its illegitimate origins. The divine burst of pure acceleration as the pedal hit the metal was its only logic. A race every few minutes (or less) kept the action at a pitch, and as the quarter-mile times shrank to a handful of neck-twisting seconds in the 1970s, the crowds grew to levels that rivalled those of baseball. Drag racing is now [in the mid-1980s] quite probably, as its boosters have long proclaimed, America's biggest spectator sport.

Custom Cars

Chronologically parallel to the hot-rod, parked side by side in places like Bob's drive-in, was the custom car. In the decade and a half that began with Truman and ended with Kennedy, the car-crazy youth of America applied time, money and maverick ingenuity to the creation of a wild public display of screaming metal. The motor car had become the dominant focus of American life; to take it and mould it into something unique was to stake a claim to the throbbing possibilities of that life, to snatch an individual identity from the huge machine press of comformity.

The custom car had hitherto been the exclusive mark of the well-heeled. The kings and princes of Europe and the rajahs of India had their Rolls-Royce, Hispano-Suiza and Mercedes-Benz limousines tailored in exquisite detail. The new nobility of America, the Hollywood movie stars, with no tradition of aristocratic reserve, no lineage of carriage and landau to draw on, could indulge in more dashing, more flamboyant, more flagrantly eye-catching exhibitions of their taste and standing. There were also more of them, and thus more individuality to be served, which allowed for the coach-building tradition to prosper in California when it died away elsewhere.

The movie colony's need to create striking images in the public and local eye supplied work for firms like the Earl Carriage Works (from which Harley Earl would later graduate to Detroit) and the Walter Murphy coachworks. Murphy's style was smooth and restrained. His windscreens had a few degrees more rake than everybody else's, and the tops of his roadsters folded down under discreet covers that created an uninterrupted curve from the back of the two-seat passenger compartment to the rear bumper. The rear wheels disappeared under wing panels, emphasising the clean, low sweep of the body. A Murphy-bodied Packard, Lincoln or Duesenberg was *the* car to own in pre-war Hollywood.

Young Bodybenders

Status, or the desire to emulate the trappings of status, cannot alone explain how the custom car progressed from being the toy of the wealthy élite to the hobby of what seemed at times like the whole post-war west coast generation. Yet the smooth, uncluttered, low-slung roadsters of Walter Murphy, Dutch Darrin and the Coachcraft company were undoubtedly the stylistic starting point for the first teenage customs. These older, established coach-builders were usually commissioned to create something like a European sports car for their clients, and their work was expensive. But after the war, adapting the golden proportions with a freer hand, a new kind of bodyshop came into being, sometimes staffed by a few old craftsmen, but more often by young, eager, apprentice bodybenders. With no fancy storefronts to maintain, they were in tune with the wishes and the means of a different sort of customer. The winged victory grille of the '49 Ford was all right for the man who had dutifully bought his war bonds, but active service merited a more glamorous and heroic contour.

This was most easily achieved by the rake of speed. When the shape of the motor car went from lean and tall to fat and round in the late 1930s, it was found that lowering the body gave a sleeker look. So began the business of cutting down the roof pillars (chopping), lowering the body on the chassis by cutting it away and rewelding (channelling), and removing a horizontal section from all the way around the middle of the body (sectioning). The voluptuous curves and bulging wings, plus the availability and good repair, of late 1930s and 1940s' Fords, Mercurys and Chevrolets made these cars the ideal subjects. In the late 1940s, people like Link Paola, Jimmy Summers and Harry Westergard took the fad, that had begun with the hot-rod and spread to regular cars, of stripping off the chrome and smoothing down the line a step farther by judicious application of the welding torch.

Come the 1950s, this essential tool cut an ever more radical and alarming path through acres of carefully ordained, annually updated Detroit sheet metal. Who were the customers of this burgeoning backyard enterprise? Initially, perhaps, a few automobile fanatics who hung out with the crowd that screeched in and out of drive-ins and ran support at the drag strips. With maybe only a ten-year-old sedanette to work on instead of a genuine hot-rod, they could nevertheless share in the action by doing to the sedanette what their peers were doing to their own souped-up highboys. Pretty soon, you were either a 'restylist', or you were nowhere. . . .

Restyling

In some areas, and at different times, the aesthetic was minimalist, in other areas at other times it was add-on. Detroit shovelled on the chrome; the kids tore it off, and then, instead, chromed their engines. Detroit introduced panoramic windscreens; the kids cut theirs down to the size of postbox slots. Restyling was the automotive equivalent of the ducktail greased-back haircut, defying modesty, decorum and engineering logic. Often it was informed by a mad sense of humour; a pseudo-beatnik craziness later exemplified by the work of Ed Roth.

The inspiration for these customs came from many sources: from the drag strip and speed trial; from the GM Motorama dream cars; but mostly from car magazines like *Hot Rod*, *Hop-Up*, *Rod & Custom* and *Honk!*, many of them a handy 5" × 8" size which could slip neatly between the covers of a high-school textbook. These magazines regularly displayed the work of the Barris brothers, Joe Bailon, Gene Winfield, Joe Wilhelm, Dean Jeffries, Gil Alaya, Neil Emory and others from the west coast homeland of the boss custom. . . .

Valley Custom in Burbank . . . specialised in the most tortuous of all restyling techniques, the horizontal section. This meant cutting out a band of metal from right round the body and its supports and joining the top and bottom halves back together. Usually, this could not easily be done in a straight line, and it required careful measurements and consideration of all the clearances inside the body. Apart from some minor detailing and the usual chrome reduction, a good section job was often all that Valley Custom did to a car; but the results, which made their name in the early 1950s, were timeless. Refined American sports coupés were now comparable to the best work of their contemporaries in Italy's Ghia and Pininfarina studios.

Sam and George Barris opened their workshop in Lynwood after learning the craft from Harry Westergard in Sacramento. In 1949, Sam Barris lowered the top of his Mercury coupé and, when the car appeared soon afterwards on the cover of *Motor Trend*, it caused a sensation. The top chop became the Barris hallmark of the early 1950s. Countless chopped Fords and Mercurys from 1941 to 1948 rolled out, looking squashed and angry, on to the forecourt of Barris Kustoms.

George ('spell it with a K') Barris was a tireless booster of the custom car, but more especially of the Barris Kustom car. While Sam, who died in the mid 1960s, supervised the workshop, George Barris was in the front office, sketching out the details of a custom with a client, organising coverage for Barris cars in magazines and exposure at the car shows. He learned the publicity value of an extravagant custom in the mid 1950s when he built the 'Golden Sahara', originally a '52 Lincoln. With its glass-covered cockpit, gullwing doors and impossibly long rear wings (not to mention TV, telephone, tape recorder and bar), the car appeared as well suited to space travel as boulevard cruising. It resembled the earlier Ford FT-Axmos dream car but was sadly unable to take advantage of Ford's envisioned compact nuclear power source.

The Golden Sahara also wore a unique pearlescent paint job. Barris had seen the pearl paint—made originally with fish scales and available only from Japan—used on a billboard. It was applied to the car over a white undercoat, sealed with clear lacquer, and then left out to dry. In the hot sunshine, the fish scales turned yellow; so Barris gold-plated the trim, and called it the Golden Sahara. The car was an unusually radical custom for Barris at the time, though later there would be many such wild essays in unconventional and exaggerated styling. . . .

No other customiser of the decade could hope to compete with Barris' gaudy entrepreneurial style. In 1955, he bought the wreck of [actor] James Dean's Porsche for $2,500, planning to re-sell each part.[1] Barris had met Dean when he customised a hot-rod for the film *Rebel Without a Cause*, and by the early 1960s, he and his cars, and most of his clients, were exclusively show business. He had always liked to cut a loud profile, and now he had the opportunity. His cars were either custom-built to be towed on trailers to the custom car shows, or custom modifications for a showbiz clientele—of which he kept a gallery of photos of car, star and Barris. If someone wanted a spectacular or zany auto for a car show or an advertising campaign or for film or TV—such as the Batmobile, based on the Lincoln Futura dream car of 1955—they came to Barris. His more famous cars were available as scale model plastic kits. and he gained pop art respectability when Tom Wolfe wrote about him in *The Kandy-Kolored Tangerine-Flake Streamline Baby*, the title of which refers to a semi-custom 1960 Chevrolet painted with Tangerine Flake, one of Barris' patent Kandy Kolors.

Commercialisation

Detroit had discovered the custom car and the hot-rod—or as they saw it, the youth market—not long before Tom Wolfe. At

1. In 1955, actor James Dean accidentally crashed his Porsche into an oncoming car and died.

first, they scratched their heads, sensing its potential size, but unable to grasp its desires. It was evidently there to be exploited because some people were already doing so. The 1960s would see the decline of the personal, driveable, home-built, self-styled fun custom and the arrival of the professional and factory special.

The custom cult had by then covered the country, with the help of magazines and car shows featuring the work of Daryl Starbird, Dave Stuckey and Bill Cushenberry in Kansas, and Dave Puhl and the Alexander brothers in Illinois. The first official car show took place at the Armory in LA's Exposition Park in 1948, sponsored by the SCTA and a Hollywood publicity agency, one of whose partners was Robert Petersen, who was about to publish the first issue of *Hot Rod* magazine. The following year, a 'hot-rod exposition' was held in Northern California; it went on to become the long-running Oakland Roadster Show. Shows such as these and the many that followed, initially loose, enthusiastic affairs, first popularised and then commercialised the custom car. . . .

At the same time, the endless and ever greater hoopla of the car shows created an accelerated cycle of custom fads. It was no longer enough to strip off the chrome, smooth down the body, and give the car a dazzling coat of paint. First, a few parts of the engine were chromed, to look like new racing goodies, then the whole engine was chromed, and then all the other bare metal was chromed, even, in the death, the entire underbody of the car!

After chrome, what? Upholstery. Everything that wasn't chromed was upholstered, even the wheel wells. The excesses of the legitimate motor industry of the late 1950s adversely affected the illegitimate industry, which was always ready to take things that much farther. . . .

Variety was now a commonplace; individuality was available over the counter in cans, decals and add-on fibreglass mouldings. The use of fibreglass allowed customisers to sell cheap, identical custom kits for a popular model of car, and even entire custom bodies. Ed Roth was the first in this field. He built his customs like a sculptor. Working in clay on a wooden buck, he would then take a mould of the finished body which could be repeated as many times as there were buyers.

Inspired by Roth's free-form 'weirdo' cars, Bruce Meyers designed a fibreglass body for a VW Beetle chassis in the early 1960s and called it the Dune Buggy. Customisers ruefully admit it was the most popular custom of all time.

Some of the top customisers began to find their individual clients dwindling and Detroit walking through the door with contracts to build show cars to lure youngsters—pre-teens who bought the Revell kits of the outlandish customs of Barris, Roth and Starbird—to things like the Ford Custom Caravans of 1963 to 1965. The show cars by then were presenting such a static and unobtainable ideal, almost a caricature of the original, that interest shifted towards the drag strip. There, at least, the cars *did* something—they were toys that worked—and what they did could be copied by anyone with enough reckless teenage nerve, which flowed at the least stimulus. The car magazines of the early 1960s had sensed this change, and began to feature drag strip results in place of lists of car show winners.

The street custom, therefore, returned to its original inspiration of speed. The mechanics of a car rather than its clothing became the focus of customising attention; although, as had happened before, the cosmetic suggestion of speed was often enough: bulging hood scoops, airfoils and spoilers, fat tyres and other performance styling 'cues' borrowed from the drags. The war babies were about to mature into affluent, car-loving customers—by the summer of 1968 half of the US population was under thirty—and drag racing had lost its delinquent taint and become a recognised sport. This was all that was needed to persuade the motor industry to make its bow in the newly defined youth market with the Pontiac GTO, the first of America's muscle cars.

Muscle Cars Versus Minis

Christopher Finch

When Japanese compact or "mini" cars were first imported to the United States in the 1960s, their small size and lack of engine power made them fairly undesirable to American buyers. However, as the sixties generation became more concerned with economy and environmental protection, the foreign compacts gained in popularity. The smaller, more efficient engines and lighter chassis weight meant that the compacts got better gas mileage than their larger American-made kin. They also seemed perfectly designed for urban environments where bigger cars were more unwieldy.

It was not only these advantages that convinced many Americans to consider foreign-built cars. As cultural historian Christopher Finch notes in the following article, the publication of Ralph Nader's *Unsafe at Any Speed* prompted Americans to question whether Detroit's automakers were producing the best (i.e., the safest and most fuel-efficient) cars. Nader, a consumer advocate, pointed to evidence that some American cars were so poorly engineered that they became dangerous to drive, and he charged that the heads of the auto industry were unconcerned about the hazards. Nader's claims gained wide media attention and pushed the auto industry to improve safety and produce its own series of fuel-efficient compact cars. However, Finch states that neither Nader's campaign nor Japanese competition would

■

force Detroit to stop producing big, gas-guzzling autos. In Finch's view, the so-called muscle cars that flooded U.S. markets in the 1960s and 1970s showed that automakers were still catering to a large section of the public that valued power and performance over economy.

Christopher Finch also authored *Rainbow*, a biography of actress Judy Garland, and is the coauthor of *Gone Hollywood*. This article is an excerpt from his book *Highways to Heaven*, a look at the impact of cars on America.

AMONG THE FOREIGN CARS APPEARING ON LA's freeways in the early sixties was a sprinkling of Japanese vehicles—Toyotas and Datsuns were the first to arrive—launched in the California market because it was known to be more adventurous, and because of the West Coast's relative proximity to Japan. At the time these cars attracted very little attention except as curiosities. Their triumph was still a decade or so away, yet their presence was a highly significant portent of things to come.

The history of the Japanese car industry to that point offered little to suggest that it would one day achieve a dominant position in the world. Datsun's roots dated back to 1912, but it did not really become a manufacturer of consequence until 1934, when the corporation was reorganized as the Nissan Motor Company Ltd. In the thirties it was best known for small cars based on the British Austin Seven. Founded in 1935, Toyota rather imaginatively took the Chrysler Airflow as the starting point for its first model and until World War II built American-style automobiles in small quantities. The war brought private-car production to a complete halt, and it did not resume until 1947, when 300 were built. For several years after the war, as Japan rebuilt, truck production took precedence over car production; 50,000 trucks had been built by 1955 as opposed to just 20,000 cars. A mere 46 cars were exported in 1956, and just 410 the following year. The majority of Toyota cars sold domestically were derivative of European models.

Nissan was building the British Austin A50 under license;

Isuzu, founded in 1937, was manufacturing another British car, the Hillman Minx; while Hino, a subsidiary of Toyota, had an arrangement with Renault to build rear-engined 4CVs. Wholly Japanese-designed cars of the period included the Datsun 1000, the Toyota Crown and the Toyota Corona, none of which was very distinguished from either a design or engineering viewpoint. Still, the Japanese car industry continued to expand rapidly, becoming the eighth largest in the world by 1960, at which point farsighted executives began to look more seriously at the potentials of the export market.

[Japan's] first effort to penetrate the United States were not especially successful, for the cars were still poorly engineered, by Detroit standards, but a foothold was established in the early sixties so that Datsun and Toyota engineers—soon to be followed by others—could gain first-hand experience of what would be needed to succeed in America. The Japanese learned their engineering lessons quickly and added an understanding of production techniques that put American manufacturers to shame. For the most part the results were well made, if derivative, cars that offered two things customers wanted: economy and reliability. The latter took a while to establish (a car must be driven for a few years before the driver knows how reliable it is). Economy, on the other hand, was evident from the first, although it didn't really come into play until events in the Middle East [when gas prices were raised in the 1970s] caused the American public to alter its entire point of view toward the automobile.

These events wouldn't happen for years, but when they did, the Japanese designers and engineers sought to learn everything they could about both the state of the art in automobile design and the needs of the motorist in a rapidly changing world.

Imitating the Mini

One of the models they turned to was a British car that never sold in America in any significant quantity, yet had an enormous influence on future car design in Japan, Europe and America: the BMC-Mini. To this day American highways are heavily traveled by its legitimate and illegitimate descendants. In the postwar decade, Europe had produced some distinguished and radical small cars—not only the VW Beetle but also the Citroën 2CV, the Renault 4CV and the Fiat 600. In 1956, after the Suez crisis had caused Europeans to consider the realities of gasoline shortages, Alec Issigonis set out to design the ultimate small car for the British Motor Corporation. Significantly, the commission came at the very time when Detroit designers were vying with one another to put larger and larger Wurlitzer organs on wheels.

Issigonis had already designed the classic Morris Minor, and now the only limitation placed on him was that he should design his supercompact vehicle around a modified version of an existing BMC engine, which meant that he could not employ an air-cooled motor (like the VW) but had to rely on a water-cooled, four cylinder unit. Actual fuel economy was largely determined by this power plant (later a number of different engines were used). The task Issigonis set himself was to create a car that in addition to providing good mileage was extremely small overall yet roomy inside, with adequate power and optimum road-holding qualities. It was his belief that even the best of the existing small cars sacrificed space for styling. For this exercise in miniaturization—the ADO 15 project—Issigonis sought to combine engineering compactness with the ultimate in minimalistic yet efficient design.

To achieve maximum passenger space it was essential to eliminate the driveshaft required in any conventional front-engine–rear-wheel-drive car. This meant either a rear-engine–rear-wheel-drive vehicle, like the Renault 4CV, or a front-engine–front-wheel-drive vehicle, like the Citroën 2CV. He chose the latter, because it would provide better weight distribution and road handling, but he went the 2CV one better, revolutionizing car layouts by mounting the engine transversely, with the transmission in the block, thus saving an enormous amount of room. He also fitted the car with ten-inch wheels, thus cutting down on wasteful fender-well space, and designed a spatially efficient suspension system, with trailing arms at the rear. As a consequence of all this, the Mini (as the ADO 15 project eventually came to be known) was only ten feet long, and Issigonis was able to boast that eight of those feet were devoted to passenger space.

Despite Issigonis's disdain for styling, the Mini was a handsomely functional-looking little car and its performance was remarkable. Even with their standard 848 cc engine, producing 34 hp, the original 1959 versions, designated Morris Mini Minor and Austin Seven, could achieve a speed of 75 mph, largely because the car weighed just 1,340 pounds, and later versions such as the 100 hp Mini Coopers were much faster. But the real glory of the Mini was its road handling and stability. If ever a car turned on a dime (or a sixpence) this was it. It was a car in which you could nip in and out of traffic as nimbly as if you were driving an MG. So good was its performance that it soon became a favorite among European rally drivers: one of the great sights of the Monte Carlo Rally in the sixties was to watch a Mini Cooper in full trim—headlights taped, covered in decals—slipstreaming behind a Lancia on the open road or zipping past a Porsche on the twisting curves of the Corniche. The Mini Cooper was so well adapted to this kind of event that it won the Monte Carlo Rally outright in 1964, 1965 and 1967, beating scores of larger and more powerful rivals.

Like the VW Beetle, the Mini had real character and enjoyed, great success in Britain as well as a number of export markets (five million were built). It was not a perfect car—although it carried four adults with reasonable comfort it barely provided trunk space for one—but its layout inspired other designers from Turin to Osaka. Perhaps the Mini was a little too small for most purposes, but it had demonstrated brilliantly how the transverse, front-mounted, front-wheel-drive motor could permit a compact car to be built with a spacious interior and superior performance and handling abilities. Issigonis himself came out with the similar but larger 1100 series in 1962, while European manufacturers were right behind, like Peugeot with the 204.

Meanwhile, in Japan, Honda was on the move, producing automobiles for the first time in 1962 after achieving international recognition with its motorcycles. The first successful Honda car was the 1966 N360, the inspiration for which was so obvious that it was immediately dubbed the Mini Honda. What makes the N360 (and hence the Mini) significant for American drivers is the fact that it was the immediate precursor of the Honda Civic, another transverse engine, front-wheel-drive small car that in layout and other particulars acknowledges the British Mini as its honorable ancestor. With the Civic, Honda would make its first impact in America, and even today's Honda Accord can trace its roots to the Mini, as can a whole rash of compact cars produced in Europe, Japan and America. The Mini started a revolution that has been felt every bit as much in the USA as in the rest of the world.

The Faulty Corvair

Back in the early sixties, however, American car manufacturers were still struggling to come to terms with the notion of the compact car. Of those launched in answer to the VW challenge, by far the most interesting was the Chevrolet Corvair, a car that might have helped prepare Detroit for the Japanese challenge but that instead set the industry back, for reasons that were not totally the fault of GM.

Few cars have received as much criticism as the Corvair. It was a near miss fraught with problems that could have been solved, given time. Certainly it was a better car than the first Japanese imports, but there was a big difference. Datsun and Toyota, with nothing to lose, could afford to take their time perfecting the product. Chevy needed immediate and continuing success in order to justify persisting with the Corvair. The immediate success was forthcoming—here was an interesting-looking car that sold in an extremely low price range—but the car's shortcomings were quickly apparent.

Ed Cole, Chevy's chief engineer, never quite acknowledged that he had taken a page out of VW's book when he designed the Corvair. Nonetheless, the car that emerged had an air-cooled engine in the tail driving the rear wheels. It did not look like a VW, however, its unit-construction body-cum-chassis design being conventionally American in appearance, though it sported a distinctive "bathtub" ridge at fender-top level and was remarkably clean and free of excessive chrome by the standards of the day. Empty it weighed 2,400 pounds, almost twice the weight of a Mini but still light compared with standard American cars. The problem was that too much of this weight was at the rear end, and as unwary drivers quickly discovered, this adversely affected the car's handling.

The front-engine, rear-wheel-drive cars Americans were used to tended to understeer, making them feel very secure to drive, if sometimes a little sluggish in response to the wheel. The Corvair was extremely prone to oversteering, so that drivers found it supersensitive to any movement of the wheel. This tendency could be kept under control to some extent by keeping front tire pressures lower than rear tire pressures, but nothing could eliminate the oversteering completely, and on slick roads even skilled drivers sometimes found that the Corvair was a terrifying vehicle to drive. When cornering at even modest speeds, on wet or icy surfaces, the heavy rear end tried to overtake the lighter front end, throwing the car out of control.

Many accidents were attributed to this handling characteristic, and critics suggested that they often had more serious consequences for the car's occupants than was necessary because of flaws in the Corvair's construction. Although unitbody construction is generally considered relatively crashproof, the notorious X-frames employed by GM made the Corvair especially vulnerable to serious damage when hit from the side, and its particular handling problems made such side hits all too likely.

Unsafe at Any Speed

Most prominent of the car's critics was Ralph Nader, who made the Corvair a prime target of his 1965 book, *Unsafe at Any Speed*. By the time the book appeared, the Corvair was already scheduled to be phased out (it survived till 1969), sales having dropped off significantly because of the public's perception of its inadequacies. The irony is that by 1964 Chevrolet had solved most of the Corvair's handling problems, so that it was no longer the same car that Nader demolished on paper.

Unsafe at Any Speed was not simply an assault on the Corvair. It was an indictment of GM's policies as a whole, and of the entire American automobile industry. As such it made many valid points, though these were blunted somewhat by the fact that Nader wrote as a man who seemed to have no feeling for the pleasures of driving. In his polemic, he is particularly biting about the conservatism of Detroit engineering and, paradoxically, acknowledges the innovations represented by the Corvair even as he points out its failings. Unfortunately, the consequence of all this was that he appears to have helped reinforce Detroit, and GM in particular, in its conservatism.

Unsafe at Any Speed may have been unintentionally instrumental in killing off adventurous compact designs for a number of years and so perhaps contributed indirectly to Detroit's failure to be prepared for the battles of the seventies.

Nader's book also had a dramatic impact upon a sizable section of the American public. The growth of import sales showed that a considerable number of Americans were prepared to doubt the wisdom of Detroit's policies; now here was a book that set out the American car industry's failings in great detail. Ever since Henry Ford revolutionized automobile production, most Americans had regarded their car builders—especially the Big Three—with something like awe. It was American enterprise at its most scintillating, weaving vast fortunes for a few while satisfying the needs and dreams of the great American public. The bosses of Ford, GM and Chrysler had been accepted as demigods—and now there was hard evidence that these men might not always have the well-being of their customers at heart. It was shocking news, and if not everyone believed all of Nader's charges, he certainly managed to sow many seeds of doubt. Were American cars the safest and best built in the world? If not, what could the consumer do about it? Nader also helped make the American car buyer self-conscious in a way that was quite novel. Perhaps it was absurd to be driving a dreamboat as big as the Ritz. Perhaps there was an alternative.

The Lure of the Muscle Cars

This is not to say that every consumer paid attention to Nader's arguments, or to suggest that Detroit lacked successes in the sixties. At Ford, for example, Lee Iacocca oversaw the development of the phenomenally successful Mustang. Originally a two-seat semi-sports-car with a relatively modest price tag, it appealed to the youthful wing of the market and sold a million between 1964, when it was introduced, and 1966. Later Mustangs, such as the Mach I, were larger four-seaters and came equipped with a variety of powerful V-8's generating up to 375 hp. The biggest of these engines gave the Mach I the capability of reaching 140 mph, making it a true muscle car.

The muscle car was an expression of everything that Ralph Nader deplored about Detroit engineering. It involved mounting a gas-hungry, high-output power plant in a conventional, standard-size chassis and wrapping it in a sedan or hard-top shell that hinted at capabilities appropriate to an Indy car. Certainly Indy cars, with their big Offenhauser and Ford V-8 engines, were one inspiration for the sixties muscle cars, but more important than Indianapolis-style racing was stock-car racing, which had become an enormous attraction after the war, first in the South and then throughout the country. It was appropriate that the archetypal family of muscle cars, the big Pontiacs, should establish its reputation with successes on the stock-car circuit.

The story of the Pontiac muscle cars began with the introduction, in 1955, of the powerful, overhead-valve, Strato-Streak V-8 engine. A few months later, Semon "Bunkie" Knudson was named head of the Pontiac Division, and he set about reversing the marque's staid image, seeking instead to capture the adventurous, youthful (or young-at-heart) driver. To do so he ordered a new approach to styling and also made an all-out assault on the stock-car circuit. Almost at once Pontiac began winning major NASCAR races, which it continued to do until 1963, when GM forbade its divisions from entering such events. Meanwhile, Royal Pontiac, a dealership based in Royal Oak, Michigan, built and raced modified Pontiacs, with great success, in the Super Stock category at national drag meets. By 1959, the marque's styling had changed dramatically (the split grille made its first appearance that year), and suddenly the Bonneville, Star Chief and even the low-end Catalina were cars to be seen in.

The Bonneville was a big car, but it was very clean compared with other Detroit products of the period. There was relative restraint in the use of chrome and a total absence of baroque excess. There were fins, but they emphasized the overall lines of the car rather than interrupting them. A certain amount of fifties *moderne* detail persisted, but basically this was a car of the sixties, and Pontiac was able to stay with the package—modifying it from year to year rather than introducing wholesale change—for two decades. By 1961, a year in which the division won thirty out of fifty-two Grand National stock-car races, Pontiac became the third-best-selling car in the country—helped, admittedly, by its newly introduced Tempest compact. In 1962 came the Grand Prix—built on the shorter Catalina wheelbase but with all the appointments of a Bonneville—then, in 1964, the GTO, a smaller yet decidedly muscular car evolved from the basic Tempest and its sportier Le Mans derivative.

This family of muscle and minimuscle cars lived on into the seventies with new arrivals like the Trans Am and the Grand Am, but it was at its peak in the sixties and in a transitional period when the industry was not at all certain where the future lay, it was a demonstration of what Detroit did best. In many ways, cars like the Bonneville and the Grand Prix were the ultimate driving machines for the newly built system of Interstates. They were not as nippy as sports cars (though they handled well), but they had the power and smoothness to take advantage of those broad, sweeping highways with their near perfect surfaces and carefully planned sightlines. And they were handsome machines whose styling stands up well in retrospect. There was nothing ridiculous about their lines, and if they borrowed from the aviation aesthetic, they did so in a less gimmicky way than their forebears had. From a sexual point of view, they were far less ambiguous than the cars of the fifties, being as straightforwardly masculine as any cars produced since the war.

With the Pontiac muscle cars the lines were drawn. If you espoused the Detroit viewpoint and understood its virtues, you drove a Bonneville or a GTO. If you were convinced by Ralph Nader's arguments, you threw up your hands in despair and wrote a letter to your congressman.

The Unsanctioned Sport of Street Racing

Pat Ganahl

What distinguishes illegal street racing from its lawful counterparts is that races are not conducted under the controlled conditions of a racetrack but on city streets, highways, and back roads. In addition, racers compete mostly for bragging rights instead of huge victory purses, though respectable sums of money often change hands at the culmination of street races. Street racing has always been an underground, unsanctioned branch of legitimate contests of speed. The popularity of contemporary films like 2001's *The Fast and the Furious* bears witness to the sport's continuing attraction to the culture's velocity junkies.

In the following article, taken from a 1985 *Hot Rod* magazine exposé on the sport, Pat Ganahl, a writer on automotive topics, offers a glimpse into the world of street racing. He provides a detailed look at several aspects of the pastime. Street racing, he states, began during the middle of the twentieth century with the increased enthusiasm for "hot rods"—highly tuned production cars modified for the purpose of enhanced performance. It was common for opponents with similarly tuned machines to challenge one another to a race to prove which was the faster of the two cars. Since then the street sport has evolved its own set of rules adhered to by most competitors.

The types of people involved in the sport, says

■

the author, have not changed much throughout the years. There is an inherent "outlaw" spirit that attracts most of the contestants to the sport and enhances the thrill of competition. They race anything with wheels that can burn up a quarter-mile of road, from trucks to motorcycles (although souped-up autos are still the main fare).

In his article Ganahl also offers some suggestions as to how the sport might distance itself from the negative associations it has acquired over the years due to its dangerous and unlawful nature. Ganahl is the author of *Ed "Big Daddy" Roth: His Life, Time, Cars, and Art; Hot Rods and Cool Customs;* and *The American Custom Car.*

I'VE DONE IT. YOU'VE DONE IT. YOUR FATHER probably did it. My mother's done it.

We're talking about short-distance, straight-line speed contest on the street. An acceleration run. A drag race. It could be pre-planned and held on a marked quarter-mile somewhere in the boonies. It might be impromptu and staged at a stoplight. Maybe it was late at night on the expressway—with another car, or just yours alone—punching it to see what she'll do. . . .

People have always street raced, and they always will.

Street racing, drag racing, and hot rodding were born together. It started with modified cars. Stock machines all run about the same. If you were driving a new '49 Chevy, you knew a '49 Ford V8 would probably beat you, and a '49 Olds overhead could whip you both. But with cars that were modified, the only way to tell whose was fastest was to race them. It is my personal conjecture that this was, in fact, the origin of the term "drag" racing. You could talk all day about how fast your A-V8 was, sitting in the garage or at the drive-in. The real test was when someone challenged, "O.K., then drag it out, and let's see what it'll do."

The only place to drag it out to, in the early days, was the street—preferably a long, wide street in a deserted area. Some early rodders found the cement Los Angeles River bed a safe place to race. Then they found the dry lakes. Then old airstrips.

The NHRA [National Hot Rod Association] finally raised drag racing from an outlaw activity to a respectable sport. But in doing so, with increasingly tight rules, classes, and indexes, they have removed the element of the unknown, that "prove it" aspect that still earmarks . . . perhaps perpetuates . . . street racing today.

The Outlaw Essence of Street Racing

Yes, street racers are outlaws. Its clandestine nature undoubtedly attracts certain participants (as well as hangers-on). And certainly there's a territorial Old West aspect to it—who's the fastest "gun" in town, and when might a "new gun" show up who's faster? The top dog, the local hero, gains a reputation, and he may be content to use it to back other competitors down verbally, if he can. Yes, lots of street racing is verbal. And, as you might expect, a key element of street racing is deception. On the one hand you have the "posers": high-dollar cars with big, blown engines and all the extras which can keep most competitors at bay without actually racing. Good ego machines. On the other hand are the "sleepers": single 4-barrel small-block machines that can run in the nines or 10's [nine- or 10-second range for a quarter-mile race]; station wagons or pickups that haul; ratty-looking cars that go fast. They make a lot of money.

Betting is an inherent aspect of street racing. Serious street racing—real street racing—is never done for free. Typical cars—the vast majority run mid-11's to mid-12's—will bet $100 to $300 each on a race. The heavy hitters, generally nine or 10-second machines, may bet $300 to $3000 each. And, of course, there are always reports of huge sums being wagered, or at least proffered (usually in heavy drug-trafficking areas). But wagering alone does not define street racing. It distinguishes it from NHRA racing (usually), but we've seen plenty of money put up on grudge races, with strip-only cars, at tracks around the country.

In my opinion, it is a combination of the outlaw image and the element of the unknown that truly distinguishes, and perhaps ultimately defines, street racing. If you know how fast two cars run, there's little point racing them, at least in the old sense of an acceleration contest. In today's "legal" drags, including brackets, cars are equalized, with speeds written right on the window. Street racers make up their own rules and keep a lot of secrets.

The Rules

The rules are unwritten, subject to change and local interpretation, and always arguable. The main rule is that things are decided beforehand: time, place, amount, starting procedure. Negotiating is a major part of this sport. The race can be run heads-up [that is, without starting lights], one car can be given so many car lengths head start (they line up with one car ahead of the other), or one car can give the other car "the go" (rather than using a starter—usually with a flashlight—the race starts when the designated car leaves). Since most cars are equipped with nitrous units, it can also be decided to race "on the motor" or "squeezing it." If a driver agrees not to use the nitrous, he must disconnect it before the race. The money is given to a third party, who usually waits at the finish line. Since there are no lights to catch early leavers or call close races, what happens if a dispute arises? Says one racer, "Some people bring guns. Normal people argue. It usually gets settled." A certain outlaw justice prevails.

Mechanically, anything goes. The general stipulation is that cars be licensed, be basically street-legal (lights, horn, wipers, etc.), and be mufflered. This helps keep the cops away. Some groups still demand that cars drive to the race site and run on street tires, but slicks and trailering have become common. As for safety equipment, that's left up to the driver. Few street racers would pass tech at a race track.

You have undoubtedly heard about street racing on Van Nuys Boulevard in Los Angeles, on Woodward in Detroit, or some similar location. That's incorrect. You couldn't possibly stage a drag race on one of these crowded city streets, especially not on a "cruise night." Instead, these were the places where street racers (and others) brought their cars to show them off . . . , and to work out the negotiating process. Once a match was set up, the cars would meet later and race at some well-removed location.

It's always been this way. In the beginning hot rodders met at a drive-in, malt shop, or someone's gas station on Friday or Saturday nights. If someone showed up with a new car, or a new modification, a challenge might arise to "drag it out" on the street. In the bigger cities, as hot rodding grew, word of such gathering places spread. More people showed up. Sometimes street races developed. But what was happening at the drive-ins and on the famous boulevards was what we call "cruising" today. Street racing was just an adjunct to it.

Now even "cruise nights" have become verticalized and organized. Street racers meet elsewhere. It's usually on an appointed night—very late at night—at a certain 24-hour hamburger joint, donut shop, or just an empty parking lot. If we told you where these meeting places were, they would be changed by the time you read this. The street racers like to get together, but they don't like to attract crowds . . . or police. The weekly late-night gatherings might or might not produce races. But if racing is to be done, it will be at some remote site. Most groups have several "strips" to choose from, and alternate their use. They might even tell the crowd they're going to one site, and then race at another. These days many big-stakes races are actually set up over the phone.

Who's a Street Racer?

Here in Los Angeles, where street racing has been going on long enough that the news media ought to know what it is, we cringe when we hear 11 o'clock reports of "Drag racers arrested (or killed) on Mulholland Drive." This well-known road that twists through the Hollywood Hills attracts ersatz road racers in wide-tired, air-dammed sporty cars. They may be racing on the street, but they're not street racers . . . definitely not drag racers. The same goes for big-dollar, exotic Banzai Runners—[Lamborghini] Countaches and turbocharged [De Tomaso] Panteras that supposedly make midnight 200-plus mile runs in less than an hour. Nor are we talking about "Cannonball" cross-country racers, cafe racers, or off-roaders. In fact, the type of street racing we're profiling here does not even include the many of us who have raced between stop-lights, punched it out on the freeway, or even met at a marked quarter-mile somewhere to see whose car was faster.

We're talking about street drag racing for money—yet another offshoot of hot rodding that has specialized and redefined itself. There are sub-groups and variations: many street racers prefer motorcycles (and run against cars); there's a group in south Los Angeles that runs only pickup trucks; there is strong ethnic involvement, especially black street racing groups; and then there are the "top enders" in Detroit who punch off from 40 or 50 mph on a deserted freeway and race until one car is clearly the winner.

Are we condoning street racing? Definitely not. We are acknowledging it; hopefully clarifying it; dispelling some misconceptions. We have given you several reasons why people street race, but we are not saying they are good reasons. Is it the money? No way—even at $1000 or more a race, you'd have a hard time recovering the cost of the car (if it was that good, no one would race you anyway). Is it the lack of available dragstrips around the country? No. . . . It may be true that some tracks discourage street race–type cars by imposing nit-picking tech regulations, not allowing grudge match-ups, or refusing to withhold times. But in actuality, lots of street race cars don't come close to meeting basic, practical safety standards; and, to be honest, a large percentage simply can't compete with well-prepared, dialed-in machines that run every week on the track. . . .

Even if you built a street racer that was fast and safe, is that any guarantee? What do you know about the construction or driving capability of the car next to you? If a car does get out of shape, there are no guardrails, no safety crew, no ambulance—in many cases no fire equipment or any type of crowd or traffic control. Racing nine or 10-second, possibly 140-mph cars under such conditions is nuts. People do get hurt—participants, spectators, unaware cross-traffic. For this reason, in many areas the police have been coming down very hard on street racers—confiscating cars and putting bystanders in jail.

What are the solutions, the alternatives? First, as in the early '50s, it would be best if the police and towns-people could help the street racers find a safe, sanctioned place to run, off the streets. . . . Second, existing dragstrips could encourage street racers with special rules or programs, perhaps on week nights. . . . Third, the street racers themselves could clean up their act by building quick, safe cars that will compete with anything on a "legal" track, and then race there. . . .

Whether we report on it or not, street racing will continue as long as there are modified cars, egos, and money to be bet.

The Folk Ritual and Folk Heroes of NASCAR

Mark D. Howell

The National Association of Stock Car Automobile Racing (NASCAR) formed in 1949 when unmodified, showroom-quality cars competed on a dirt track in Charlotte, North Carolina. Today, the restrictions on NASCAR vehicles have changed dramatically. The automobiles that compete in the modern Winston Cup Series are among the world's most sophisticated machines. Their performance abilities far exceed those of even the most powerful production car. With race cars hurtling at speeds in excess of two hundred miles per hour, the laws of physics acting upon the driver are unlike anything most people have the opportunity to experience. Large support teams work gruelingly to simply keep the car and driver in the race. Sometimes their efforts are not enough. Terrible crashes like the one that killed legendary racer Dale Earnhardt Sr. in 2001 are sobering reminders of the sport's dangerous nature.

When a NASCAR racing event is held, thousands of spectators from all over the country fill the grandstands. These are augmented by tens of thousands watching on television. Car and driver loyalty among fans is known to supersede even their religious and political affiliations. NASCAR racing is undoubtedly one of the most popular American sports of all time.

Mark D. Howell, a cultural historian in the de-

■

Mark D. Howell, *Moonshine to Madison Avenue: A Cultural History of the NASCAR Winston Cup Series*. Bowling Green, OH: Bowling Green State University Popular Press, 1997. Copyright © 1997 by Bowling Green State University Popular Press. All rights reserved. Reproduced by permission of Wisconsin Press.

partment of American thought and language at
Michigan State University, argues in the following
article that there are various psychological forces at
work in creating such widespread cultural zeal for
NASCAR racing. Howell considers the Winston Cup
Series as a cultural ritual that provides the spectator
with a means to safely and vicariously experience an
exciting world of speed and danger. In addition,
Howell postulates that NASCAR drivers have become modern-day folk heroes whose appeal is based
on performing feats of cleverness and amazing physical endurance.

Another aspect of their folk-hero mystique is
their "outlaw" image. NASCAR can trace its roots to
the illicit, grassroots liquor-running trade of the mid–
twentieth century. Men who drove highly tuned production cars and outsmarted local law enforcement
agencies to bring bootleg whiskey to the poor southern working man color the sport's past history. Some
successful drivers of the modern organization, such as
Dale Earnhardt Sr., picked up this antiauthoritarian
image (and were marketed as such by their sponsors),
generating a huge fan base of white males who
sought to identify with the character traits of the des-
perado without really having to challenge the law.
The enthusiasm embodied by such fans does not go
unnoticed or unappreciated by the NASCAR organization, and so the sport has little trouble acquiring
and maintaining its devotees.

STOCK CAR DRIVERS, LIKE THE HORSEMEN OF
the American West, occupy a special place within American
culture. Just as frontier scouts and cowboys have become a ro-
manticized part of our national history, Winston Cup drivers
have become symbols of the character traits that Americans
admire. The meaning of the NASCAR Winston Cup Series,
and its role in the world of professional sports, must be ana-
lyzed, interpreted, and treated as an important component of
life in the United States. . . .

NASCAR Winston Cup racing is . . . a cultural ritual. It addresses the nature of American society—a society occupied with automobiles, technology, consumption of material goods, and competition. Those who participate in the sport are folk heroes and media celebrities; they are professional athletes and daredevils. The Winston Cup stock car driver is considered fearless, intuitive, physically adroit, and emotionally cool. Like the scouts who tempted death along the Great Plains, NASCAR drivers tempt death on high-banked ovals at speeds of better than 200 miles per hour. There is little difference between dodging bullets along a trail in Wyoming and dodging concrete walls along a straightaway at Daytona; both have the power to stop a man quickly and permanently.

Beyond the Ordinary

What makes the stock car driver so unique within American culture is his ability to use and manipulate technology. This is not unlike the frontiersman who gained acclaim for his abilities to shoot, hunt, track game, and ride. Whereas the majority of Americans climb into their cars for their daily commute to work, the Winston Cup driver climbs into his car to try and defy principles of physics and engineering. The stock car driver tries to test every aspect of the 3,400-pound machine under him: its engine, its handling characteristics, and its durability. While the daily commuter worries about spilling coffee on his dress clothes, the NASCAR driver worries about keeping his car on its wheels. . . .

Because their talents transcend average human ability, NASCAR Winston Cup drivers are considered heroes. They do something that most of us can only think about. We drive every day, but our arena is the highway, the city street, the crowded parking lot near our office. Stock car drivers, like the frontier heroes of old, challenge their environment and test themselves against the unknown. The rest of us simply stand by to observe and admire. These brave men become the subject of our conversations as we dream of their talents and tell stories about their accomplishments. Admirers of such men elevate these individuals to folk hero status. They become symbols for our society and our lives; they set the standards that we wish we could follow.

Folk heroes often come from the ranks of professional athletes. Even touring entertainers like Buffalo Bill and Annie Oakley followed this pattern—their talents in the horse ring earned them many admirers who followed their exploits and paid to see them perform in person. As sports turned professional and became more recognized as popular entertainment, athletes became a central part of our culture. Athletes soon became the focus of our popular folklore as Americans began to swap stories about the lives, talents, and accomplishments of these newfound celebrities. . . .

Facts and Fictions

Heroes, whether they are sports figures, politicians, or some other socially significant individual, exist in two separate spheres. As the age-old dilemma of history goes—what people did and what we *say* they did are often two different things. Such is the nature of folklore; an emphasis on people—the "folk"—makes it a circumspect way of gathering data about important topics. The advantage of human fallibility is that it opens doors to us regarding the *why* and *how* certain people are remembered as folk heroes, which is often more important than the issue of *who* is considered a hero in the first place.

Examples of this are not hard to find. Christopher Columbus was remembered as the man who "discovered" America, and praised as such, yet we now know the details of his travels. The "facts" about Columbus and his journey in 1492 are different than the "fiction" that has been committed to public memory. Atrocities toward the Arawaks who encountered Spanish explorers have been conveniently overlooked. Even Charles Lindbergh, the first to fly across the Atlantic Ocean alone, can be interpreted in two distinct ways: he was the "Lone Eagle" in 1927, but he was also recipient of the Order of the German Eagle [a Nazi German award] in 1938. . . . At some point, these memories, these "facts" and their varying interpretations, or "fictions," have become part of our history. Ordinary people remind each other about these stories, these events, these famous people, and the tales get revised every time they are retold. The revisions come from our culture, from the things we consider important at any particular time in our lives, and these revisions color our history until it is time to tell the stories again. . . .

How Modern-Day Heroes Are Made

Winston Cup stock car drivers, like other professional athletes, become folk heroes because they spend most of their careers—and personal lives—under a media microscope. The general public learns far more than it rightly deserves to know. Regular consumers of sports news learn where athletes live, how much money they make, details about private affairs, and explicit information regarding the not-so-private ones. Professional athletes become news items away from the field of competition, especially given their wealth and social status. They can also earn column inches and airtime for a lapse in personal judgment. . . . Such is the situation for a man or woman making millions of dollars each year from playing a game in front of paying audiences.

We buy seats to stadiums and arenas, we thrill to the exploits of an individual participant, we find ourselves fascinated with a player, and we search out more information about the player-turned-person. By learning intimate details about the athlete's life, we can then associate ourselves with him or her; we compensate for his or her athletic ability by learning about the athlete's faults and foibles. Michael Jordan thrills us with his ability to slam dunk a basketball, but he also pacifies us with the knowledge that he was once cut from his junior high school basketball team. Suddenly the legend seems more normal, more mediocre. Suddenly the professional athlete seems like us, a revelation introduced from within the society we live in.

Societies utilize folklore and storytelling to enhance the mystique of revered figures like professional athletes, often exaggerating or highlighting less well-known events to enhance their public images. . . . The stories we tell about sports heroes reaffirm who we are as fans and citizens, and who the hero is as an entertainer and a cultural symbol.

Many stories serve as a means of explaining an individual's greatness. Sheer talent is rarely enough; there is often some life experience that affects the creation of a sports hero. Such is the case with Junior Johnson, whose tenacity on the racetrack was formed, according to sports folklore, from years of doing battle against federal agents on the backroads of North Carolina. Racing lore also credits Johnson with originating the "bootlegger's turn," a move used during races when a car gets spun in an opposite direction. Whether Junior Johnson created such a move or not is left up to debate. What makes this an important issue is that it has become a part of NASCAR folklore—a story told across generations of racing fans—and Johnson has become a legend in the process. Legions of stock car followers learn these stories, interpret them, and take from them the cultural contexts they consider to be most important at that particular time.

Stock car racing is a fertile field for the creation of such folk legends. It is a sport that thrived on word-of-mouth in the years before mainstream media accepted it as a major force in American athletics. Stories circulated from dirt tracks throughout the country by way of garages and schoolyards, over gas pumps and barstools. The exploits of local drivers who battled for glory at shrines like Darlington and Daytona became part of auto racing lore. As those drivers—men like Tim and Fonty Flock, Curtis Turner, Red Byron, Lee Petty, and Junior Johnson—worked their way from dirt to asphalt, their stories reflected some of the issues emerging from NASCAR's infancy. Moonshine haulers became athletes, recognized names throughout the country, and their stories—now a part of NASCAR folklore—addressed the culture from which they came. . . .

The Origins of NASCAR

The outlaw element of stock car racing derived from [the] early days of NASCAR. These "outlaws" were already the subjects of regional folklore: Curtis Turner, a teenaged liquor-hauler-turned-lumber-tycoon, and Junior Johnson, arrested by federal agents while standing guard at his daddy's still. These stories reflect a variety of cultural elements central to life in the American Southeast, primarily aspects involving self-reliance and personal economic survival. . . .

Hollywood and American popular culture immortalized the legend of Junior Johnson by translating his story onto film. *The Last American Hero*, a 1973 motion picture by Twentieth Century Fox, presented the saga of Johnson and his family's moonshine business in contemporary terms. "Junior Jackson" hauls the corn liquor made by his father and winds up discovering stock car racing, eventually becoming a winning driver on the national circuit. The boy from the mountains makes good, and leaves bootlegging behind to find his fortune in professional sport. . . .

The rural, southern nature of Winston Cup stock car racing is responsible for America's initial conception of drivers and their place within the domination of professional sport. Some of the earliest stock car racers, according to folklore of the rural South, were men who hauled moonshine through the mountains of North Carolina during the 1930s and 1940s. They faced arrest and imprisonment if caught; this provided them with the inspiration to make their automobiles the fastest and strongest available. . . .

Early stock car races were held on the backroads of rural North Carolina between two men who decided to see which one had the fastest car in that particular area. Such "wheelmen" as these quickly gained a following as local racing heroes, whether they competed on or off of the track. These early challenges expanded onto the dirt horse-racing tracks of southern fairgrounds, where several moonshine runners could race each other without fear of getting caught by authorities. What the moonshiners wanted was an opportunity to test their driving abilities at an equitable venue. Each ran independently when on the roads hauling corn liquor—the main objective there was to not get arrested. Bragging rights were hard to settle without head-to-head contests, and fields of cars were unable to run effectively at night on the backroads. It was not until 1949 that these amateur race car drivers had a chance to compete against each other—and other skilled competitors—under regulated and lawful conditions.

The first official NASCAR Strictly Stock event was held on June 19, 1949, on a ¾-mile dirt track at the Charlotte Fairgrounds. A driver had to run under NASCAR regulations, which stated that cars were to be "new model," or no more than three years old and of showroom quality. This meant the cars were to be entirely stock, except that headlights could be taped over and hub caps and mufflers removed. For moonshiners, this was automatically a step backward since they drove cars modified to outrun the law. Moonshine cars were not "stock," even though they were used on open roads, and so deemed illegal according to NASCAR. In this new "Strictly Stock" division, victory would be based on the skills of each individual driver, not on the modifications of his car. This race marked the beginning of what is today known as the NASCAR Winston Cup Series. . . .

NASCAR in the Television Age

Because Winston Cup races are broadcast live on national television, it is essential that cultural symbols and images are made a part of the television coverage. It provides a means by which the networks involved can have an impact on the largest number of viewers possible. Giving the audience culturally significant images is the best way that programmers can capture—and maintain—a large and loyal national audience. Some of these images include close-ups of flags (both American and Confederate) and women and children (symbolic of family in a male-dominated sport).

Hundreds of millions of television viewers watch Winston Cup races on TV each year. Such huge numbers demonstrate the effect that television coverage can have on a national scale. Just as popular television shows can affect the behavior of viewers, as in clothing styles, hair styles, or colloquial language, it is possible that cultural symbols can also be projected upon a national audience for their acceptance and acquisition. . . .

Certain stories about folk heroes are better if told in regionally relevant terms. For example, when Jeff Gordon won the inaugural Brickyard 400 at Indianapolis Motor Speedway in August of 1994, the news media emphasized his ties to the Midwest. Here was a 23-year-old from Indiana excelling in a sport born and bred in the American South. No matter that Gordon had been running stock cars since 1991, winning in Grand National and Winston Cup competition at tracks like Daytona and Charlotte; what mattered most was that a young man from America's Heartland had won a stock car race at the nation's most revered speedway. As Steve Waid put it in the *Winston Cup Scene* of August 11, 1994, "The favorite son of Pittsboro, Ind., the driver they call 'The Kid,' becomes part of auto racing lore by winning the first NASCAR Winston Cup race ever run at the venerated Indianapolis Motor Speedway." Ironically enough, the national media got so caught up in Gordon's win, many in the press neglected to say that Jeff Gordon was really a native of California, spending the early years of his life near Vallejo. His move to Indiana came because it was where a 13-year-old could purchase and drive a sprint car. From there, Jeff Gordon moved into NASCAR racing. . . .

Dale Earnhardt as the Archetypal Folk Hero

Today NASCAR drivers are marketed and promoted by major corporations, and the corporate image projected is often the one turned into contemporary folklore. Take, for example, the image of Dale Earnhardt [Sr.]. His father, the late Ralph Earnhardt, was a peer of Curtis Turner and Junior Johnson; his rough-and-tumble reputation made him a successful and revered driver throughout the Southeast. Dale grew up in this environment, watching his father beat and bang against the best of them on his way to a NASCAR Modified championship. Dale Earnhardt knew that he was going to be a race car driver like his father, and that is precisely what he became.

Dale Earnhardt's climb to championship status, however, was a tough one. The stories of his struggle used to be part of the man's personal history, part of Earnhardt's personal narrative. Failed marriages, working a variety of day jobs, and living in near poverty while trying to make it as a stock car driver were all stories of Dale Earnhardt's life experiences. Now those stories are a part of Winston Cup folklore, reflecting the challenges, hardships, and sacrifices required of a national champion. Look at Winston Cup racing, and you find stories of the obstacles all drivers had to clear.

Stories of challenge and hardship like these have circulated throughout the grandstands and garage stalls, many carried by the media and interpreted by those who hear or read them. Personal narrative is the fuel that drives the wheels of emerging folklore, and the lessons we learn from such stories make up the fabric of the NASCAR Winston Cup Series. Many times these stories will conjure up images that stock car fans will identify with, providing them with a connection that brings the spectator one step closer to the sport. . . .

The image of Dale Earnhardt is . . . symbolic of attitudes within America. [*Sports Illustrated* writer] Ed Hinton wrote about "the general surliness of our society, a public with an attitude that mirrors Earnhardt's attitude." This, according to Charlotte Motor Speedway's president and general manager

H.A. "Humpy" Wheeler, might explain Earnhardt's appeal to a larger, more casual racing audience:

> Earnhardt is the resurrected Confederate soldier. . . . Where [Richard] Petty was always compliant, Earnhardt will stand his ground and say, "I'm not going to do that." And the people who love him are the people who are told, every day, what to do and what not to do, and they've got all those rules and regulations to go by. That just draws them closer to him.

Earnhardt's attitude toward the Winston Cup lifestyle makes him a symbol of individualism in a sport where following sponsors' (and NASCAR's) orders is expected. The rebellious nature of Earnhardt, a reminder of stock car racing's other free spirits, Curtis Turner and Tim Richmond, provides race fans with a model to emulate—at least subconsciously—in times of personal and occupational stress and uncertainty. In this sense, Dale Earnhardt is much more than a Winston Cup driver and media celebrity; he projects cultural meaning through his behavior in the world of professional sport. He is a central figure in the history of NASCAR and its evolution into one of America's most popular spectator sports.

The history of the NASCAR Winston Cup Series in and of itself is expressive of numerous issues: development of the automobile, Prohibition, labor organizations, advertising, and mass media to name a few. More important, however, the sport of stock car racing expresses other, more deeply rooted elements of American life. It is an activity that operates as a text— a guidebook that embodies some basic rules for American living and some fundamental ideas that help us cope with the responsibilities and problems of American civilization. . . .

Corporation and Fan Support

Americans raise individuals to heights of national recognition and try to emulate them. In some cases, we are inspired by figures who have achieved something that we ultimately want to achieve ourselves, as in the case of a movie star or a professional athlete. In other cases, we admire people whose lives and personalities reflect our own.

Automobile racing, in general, is a sport of personalities

and machinery. It is a sport of almost limitless variables. The driver is the figure at the center of the team, even though his or her role is actually fairly secondary. Today's stock car drivers work with high-dollar contracts and press agents. Media attention is constant, with newspapers, magazines, television, and radio all muscling in for a piece of the sport. Stock car racing used to be a matter of family and community; today it is a matter of a family being associated with Fortune 500 companies and CEOs. Sponsorship has become the key to racing success, as all too many independent drivers have learned the hard way.

The subculture of the NASCAR Winston Cup Series lives off deep roots. Its legions of fans are legendary and seriously loyal to drivers, automobile manufacturers, and sponsors. These are the people who purchase the tickets and the T-shirts, the caps, and the collectibles. They write letters to racing publications when they feel their driver has been wronged. They buy personal messages to offer support and/or praise when their driver needs a pat on the back. These are the people who comprise the backbone of Winston Cup stock car racing.

NASCAR and its many racing teams recognize this fact. Stock car drivers realize that fans make it possible for them to race for a living. The sponsors realize that fans will buy their products, with almost blind loyalty, simply because of their Winston Cup connections. This is the reason why stock car drivers still give their autographs for free, while "mainstream" athletes charge for their signatures at card shows or memorabilia exhibitions. Stock car drivers realize that fans make their race cars go 'round, that dedicated and happy fans make the NASCAR Winston Cup Series a real force within the realm of professional sports.

3

EXAMINING *POP* CULTURE

Cultural Myths
and Symbols

The Myth of
Henry Ford as
Folk Hero

James J. Flink

"More was written about Henry Ford during his lifetime, and he was more often quoted, than any figure
in American history," asserts social science professor
and automobile historian James J. Flink in his analy-
sis of Ford as an American folk hero. Flink goes on to
say that rural America (which comprised a third of
the nation in the early 1900s) venerated the automotive giant and "thought Henry Ford a greater emancipator of the common man than Abraham Lincoln."
The reasons for this are part of Ford's mythology,
which as Flink says, was chiefly perpetuated by Ford
himself. Ford is often credited with introducing the
automobile to America and initiating mass production techniques in the auto industry. These techniques lowered the prices of automobiles, making
them affordable for rural Americans. And since Ford's
cars were selling at the turn of the century, mass production also gave his blue-collar workers a raise in
wages ($5 for an eight-hour day). Both of these bene-
fits earned Ford the praise of the poorer classes. The
ubiquity of Ford's Model T car, nicknamed "the
people's car," further made the automaker appear to
be the champion of the common man. Ford also
gained the support of middle-class businessmen, who
lauded Ford for his industry acumen and agreed with
Ford that big business was best for America—that ef-

■

James J. Flink, *The Car Culture*. Cambridge, MA: The MIT Press, 1975. Copyright
© 1975 by The Massachusetts Institute of Technology. All rights reserved. Reproduced by permission.

ficiently run industry was a better embodiment of national ideals than the best-run government.

In the following selection Flink challenges the mythic stature of Henry Ford by exposing the falsehoods of his claims to fame. Flink points out that Ford was not the inventor of the automobile in America, nor was he the first industrialist to use assembly-line automation to streamline production. Furthermore, despite the populist image that his admirers cultivated, Ford was, according to Flink, an elitist who believed the average working person was lazy, docile, and without ambition. Yet the myth of Ford as an innovator and supporter of the blue-collar wage earner persists in the nation's folklore because textbooks continue to praise Henry Ford's ingenuity, industriousness, and compassion for the common man—traits that are still promoted in automobile industry advertisements today.

Flink is the author of three books on the automobile in America: *The Car Culture; America Adopts the Automobile, 1895–1910;* and *The Automobile Age.* He has also written several articles on the subject.

THE IDOLIZATION OF HENRY FORD AS A SYMBOL of differing national aspirations reflected the universal human tendency to personify the impersonal forces of history—thus simplistically reducing the complexities of historical processes down to a dramatic parade of symbolic heroes and villains. Consequently, much of what passes for history in textbooks as well as in the popular imagination is merely the perpetuation of culturally meaningful, but misleading, myths. Henry Ford himself recognized this in the often misquoted, unwittingly sophisticated statement he made to Charles N. Wheeler, a newspaper reporter, in 1916: "History is more or less bunk."...

One of Many Carmakers

The great disservice that Henry Ford did to written history—ironic for a man who complained to reporters as late as 1940 that history "isn't even true"—was that his extreme egocentrism deluded him into becoming the chief progenitor of a cult of personality based upon heroic myths. He lost no opportunity to claim personal credit for both the low-priced reliable car and the mass-production techniques that together revolutionized American life. He also cultivated the public image that the success of the giant Ford Motor Company was entirely due to his individual genius. A Chicago newspaper editor once aptly quipped, "One need not mention Ford—he mentions himself." Ford doted on articles about himself and religiously amassed for posterity what is probably the largest collection of personal data ever accumulated by an American businessman.

The man who most strongly opposed the preposterous claim that George B. Selden invented the gasoline automobile ironically came to fall just short of making the same claim for himself. As late as 1963 the Ford Motor Company advertised: "Henry Ford had a dream that if a rugged, simple car could be made in sufficient quantity, it would be cheap enough for the average family to buy." But the truth is that Ford's idea of "a car for the great multitude" was a generally held expectation, assumed to be inevitable from the introduction of the motor vehicle in the United States. Ransom E. Olds and Thomas B. Jeffery were the most important among several other automobile manufacturers who attempted prematurely to implement the idea while Henry Ford was still absorbed with building racing cars. The basic elements of automotive technology embodied in the Model T were invented and developed by scores of other automotive pioneers. The constituents of mass production—described by Henry Ford in the *Encyclopaedia Britannica* as "the focusing upon a manufacturing project of the principles of power, accuracy, economy, system, continuity, speed, and repetition"—were all well-known aspects of an evolving American manufacturing tradition by the time they were adapted to the Model T.

Recognition that the Ford Motor Company led the industry in developing the mass-produced and, as a consequence, low-priced car should not obscure the fact that Ford's effort to increase output greatly in the 1908–1913 period was far from unique. Many of Ford's competitors attempted to cut manufacturing costs and capitalize on the insatiable demand for motorcars by working out similar solutions to their common production problems. . . .

Ford's Assembly Line

Charles E. Sorensen, who was in charge of production at Ford, was keenly aware that the contribution of the Ford Motor Company to mass production lay almost entirely in its refinement of the integration and coordination of the process of final assembly. Sorensen knew that "Eli Whitney used interchangeable parts when making rifles in the early days of the Republic; and in the early days of this century Henry Leland . . . applied the same principles in the first Cadillac cars. Overhead conveyors were used in many industries, including our own. So was substitution of machine work for hand labor. Nor was orderly progress of the work anything new; but it was new to us at Ford until Walter Flanders showed us how to arrange our machine tools at the Mack Avenue and Piquette plants [in Michigan]." The only significant contribution that Sorensen claimed for the Ford Motor Company was "the practice of moving the work from one worker to another until it became a complete unit, then arranging the flow of these units at the right time and the right place to a moving final assembly line from which came a finished product. Regardless of earlier uses of some of these principles, the direct line of succession of mass production and its intensification into automation stems directly from what we worked out at Ford Motor Company between 1908 and 1913."

The moving assembly line at Ford was conceived one Sunday morning in July 1908 at the Piquette Avenue plant during the last months of Model N production. The parts needed for assembling a car were laid out in sequence on the floor; a frame was next put on skids and pulled along by a towrope until the axles and wheels were put on, and then rolled along in notches until assembled. However, this first experiment to assemble a car on a moving line did not materialize into a moving-belt final assembly line at Ford until 1913 because the extensive changes in plant layout and procedures "would have indefinitely delayed Model T production and the realization of Mr. Ford's long cherished ambition which he had maintained against all opposition."

There was general agreement in the automobile industry that the sixty-acre Highland Park plant that Ford opened on January 1, 1910, to meet the huge demand for the Model T possessed an unparalleled factory arrangement for the volume production of motorcars and that its well-lighted and well-ventilated buildings were a model of advanced industrial construction. By 1914 about 15,000 machines had been installed. Company policy was to scrap machines as fast as they could be replaced with improved types, and by 1912 the tool department was constantly devising specialized new machine tools that would increase output. The elementary time and motion studies begun at the Piquette Avenue plant were continued and in 1912 led to the installation of continuous conveyor belts to bring materials to the assembly lines. Magnetos, motors, and transmissions were assembled on moving lines by the summer of 1913. After the production from these subassembly lines threatened to flood the final assembly line, a moving-chassis assembly line was installed. It reduced the time of chassis assembly from twelve and a half hours in October to two hours and forty minutes by December 30, 1913. . . .

The mass-production techniques developed at Highland Park to meet the demand for the Model T became synonymous in the mind of the public with Henry Ford's name. These techniques were widely publicized and described in detail, most definitively by Horace L. Arnold and Fay L. Faurote. Ford's competitors in the automobile industry quickly installed moving-belt assembly lines, too. But the Ford Motor Company set the pace and direction of a new social order based on mass production and mass personal automobility until the early 1920s, when Hudson probably surpassed and other automobile manufacturers began to equal Highland Park's efficiency in production.

The evidence is unequivocal that both the Model T and the Ford mass-production methods, in [biographer Reynold M.] Wik's words, "represented the efforts of a team of engineers, rather than the inspiration of one man, Henry Ford." C. Harold Wills, the chief engineer, and Joseph Galamb head a long list of Ford employees whose collective efforts were more significant than Henry Ford's inspiration in creating the Model T. Charles E. Sorensen, his assistant Clarence W. Avery, William C. Klann, and P.E. Martin deserve the lion's share of credit for the moving-belt assembly line worked out at Highland Park, while the specialized machinery was designed by a staff of dozens of engineers headed by Carl Emde. . . .

Ford's Opinions of the Common Man

The image of Henry Ford as a progressive industrial leader and champion of the common people that Americans clung to during the 1920s was incredibly incongruent with much of the philosophy of industry expounded by Ford himself in *My Life and Work* (1922), *Today and Tomorrow* (1926), and *My Philosophy of Industry* (1929).

Far from identifying with the Jeffersonian yeoman farmer glorified in Populist rhetoric, Henry Ford looked forward to the demise of the family farm. As a youth Ford had hated the drudgery of farm labor, and he longed to rid the world of unsanitary and inefficient horses and cows. But the Model T was conceived as "a farmer's car" less because Ford empathized with the plight of the small farmer than because any car designed for a mass market in 1908 had to meet the needs of a predominantly rural population. "The old kind of farm is dead," Ford wrote in 1926. "We might as well recognize that fact and take it as a starting point for something better." He looked forward in 1929 to the day when "large corporations . . . will supersede the individual farmer, or groups of farmers will combine to perform their work in a wholesale manner. This is the proper way to do it and the only way in which economic freedom can be won."

Henry Ford viewed the common man with a cynical, elitist paternalism, fundamentally at odds with the equalitarian Populist philosophy he supposedly represented. "We have to recognize the unevenness in human mental equipment," said Ford. "The vast majority of men want to stay put. They want to be led. They want to have everything done for them and have no responsibility." Ford admitted that the thought of repetitive labor was "terrifying to me. I could not do the same thing day in and day out, but to other minds, perhaps to the majority of minds, repetitive operations hold no terrors." He believed that "the average worker . . . wants a job in which he does not have to put forth much physical exertion—above all, he wants a job in which he does not have to think . . . for most purposes and most people, it is necessary to establish something in the way of a routine and to make most motions purely repetitive—otherwise the individual will not get enough done to live off his exertions."

A journalist asked Ford in 1923, "What about industrial democracy?" "The average employee in the average industry is not ready for participation in the management," Ford answered. "An industry, at this stage of our development, must be more or less of a friendly autocracy." This cynical, elitist paternalism pervaded the Ford Motor Company even during the early years that Ford's admirers peg as its brightest and most progressive. . . .

In Ford's philosophy of industry, the key figure remained the entrepreneurial capitalist, whose supposed superior intelligence enabled him to organize production more and more efficiently through the continual reinvestment of his profits in improved machinery. It followed axiomatically for Ford that this industrial superman had the unquestionable prerogative to determine what were fair profits, wages, and prices free from any interference by the government, workers, or consumers. If the superman erred he would be punished by the classical economists' bogeymen, the invisible hand of the market and the unenforceable law of supply and demand. . . .

The Capitalist and the Social Good

Although the Ford five-dollar, eight-hour day entailed recognition that mass consumption was a necessary corollary of mass production, Henry Ford nevertheless was still committed to most of the beliefs and values of a production-oriented society and economy. He did come to see that mass production made the worker "more a buyer than a seller," and that "the 'thrift' and 'economy' ideas have been overworked." But Ford abhorred waste and remained committed to the central tenet of a production-oriented society and economy—the work ethic. "Thinking men know that work is the salvation of the race, morally, physically, socially," claimed Ford. "Work does more than get us our living: it gets us our life."

Seeing the cure for poverty and want in terms of more efficient production, Ford held that "hiring two men to do the job of one is a crime against society" and that mass production, despite the great increase in output per worker, would always continue to create more jobs than it destroyed. To Ford, overproduction was a theoretical possibility that would mean "a world in which everybody has all that he wants." Ford feared that "this condition will be too long postponed." Nonetheless, he believed that, in the automobile industry, "We do not have to bother about overproduction for some years to come, provided our prices are right." Meanwhile, neither charity nor drones had any place in Henry Ford's conception of the good society and economy: "Fully to carry out the wage motive, society must be relieved of non-producers. Big business, well organized, cannot serve without repetitive work, and that sort of work instead of being a menace to society, permits the coming into production of the aged, the blind, and the halt. It takes away the terrors of old age and illness. And it makes new and better places for those whose mentality lifts them above repetitive work."

Mass Production and the Worker

Mass production meant that neither physical strength nor the long apprenticeship required to become a competent craftsman was any longer a prerequisite for industrial employment. The creativity and experience on the job that had been valued in the craftsman were considered liabilities in the assembly-line worker. . . .

Mass production had two clear benefits from the point of view of the worker. One was that the resulting higher wages and lower prices raised the worker's standard of living appreciably. The other was that new opportunities for remunerative industrial employment were opened to the immigrant, the Black migrant to the northern city, the physically handicapped, and the educable mentally retarded. For the machine did not discriminate and did not demand substantial training, physical strength, education, or intelligence from its operator. Except for the outspokenly anti-Semitic articles published in his *Dearborn Independent*, for which Ford publicly apologized in 1927, no employer was more immune than Henry Ford from the prevailing ethnic, racial, and social prejudices of his day. "Our employment office does not bar a man for anything he has previously done," said Ford. "He is equally acceptable whether he has been in Sing Sing or at Harvard and we do not even inquire from which place he has graduated. All that he needs is the desire to work.". . .

The demands of the assembly line also put a premium on youth. [Historians Allan] Nevins and [Frank E.] Hill relate that "the bosses had a natural liking for young, vigorous, quick men not past thirty-five. Experienced hands past that age, if they did not possess some indispensable skill, were thus often the first to be dismissed and the last to be re-engaged.". . .

Social Impact of Mass Production

Mass production influenced many changes in the American way of life that were perceptible by the mid-1920s. Respect for age and parental authority was undercut in blue-collar families as sons became more valued as workers than their fathers. Being male lost some status because, theoretically at least, women could now be employed in industry on the same footing as men. Although the employment of women did not occur on any significant scale until industry experienced grave labor shortages in World War II, the democratization of the American family was furthered by mass production. The role of the housewife changed from that of a producer of many household items to a consumer of ready-made clothes, prepared foods, and electrical appliances, necessitating that she be given more control over the family budget. In addition, the mass-produced family car widened her range of associations beyond the narrow sphere of the home.

From the perspective of traditional American values, the impact of mass production on the worker was debilitating. The individual became an anonymous, interchangeable robot who had little chance on the job to demonstrate his personal qualifications for upward mobility into the echelons of management. Thus the American myth of unlimited individual social mobility, based on ability and the ideal of the self-made man, became frustrating impossibilities for the assembly-line worker. As the job became a boring, dead-ended treadmill to escape from rather than a calling in which to find fulfillment, leisure began to assume a new importance for the assembly-line worker. The meaning of work, long sanctified in the Protestant Ethic, was reduced to monetary remuneration. The value of thrift and personal economy became questionable, too, as mass consumption became an inevitable corollary of mass production.

Youthful Freedom: The Symbolic Connection Between Cars and Rock and Roll

E.L. Widmer

In the following article E.L. Widmer charts the co-evolution of the automobile and rock and roll music in the 1950s. According to Widmer, cars and rock music have a natural affinity because both are symbols of youth and freedom. To young people in the 1950s cars offered independence, provided a means of personal expression, and symbolized the growing economic power of the post–World War II teenage population. They also provided young couples with a means to engage in sexual exploration away from the watchful eyes of adults. It is no wonder, Widmer writes, that rock and roll music—a sexually charged form of rhythm and blues—often eroticized the automobile in the lyrics of such hit songs of the 1950s as "Rocket 88" and "Maybellene."

Besides emphasizing the sexual overtones of car songs, Widmer suggests that car ownership also befit the rock star image that was first cultivated by performers in the 1950s. Using the King of Rock and Roll as one of his models, Widmer asserts that Elvis Presley's penchant for collecting and driving cars re-

■

E.L. Widmer, "Crossroads: The Automobile, Rock and Roll, and Democracy," *Roadside America: The Automobile in Design and Culture*, edited by Jan Jennings. Ames: Iowa State University Press, 1990.

flected his new economic status. Presley had been born poor but became a wealthy rock and roll star. Purchasing automobiles was a way of symbolizing his own achievement—a means of showing himself and others that he had succeeded in overcoming his impoverished background. Since Presley's day, other rock idols have shared this belief that ownership of cars and other luxury items is one of the rewards, and outright indicators, of fame and success.

When Widmer wrote this piece in the early 1990s he was a PhD candidate at Harvard University. He has contributed articles to *Harvard Magazine*, the *Boston Globe*, *Spy*, and other publications.

THOMAS EDISON INVENTED THE RECORDING cylinder in 1877, only to see it superseded by Emile Berliner's flat phonograph disc in 1895, a year before Henry Ford knocked down the wall of his landlord's barn to push his motorized quadricycle into the street and history. Since that inventive era and the nearly twinned births of automotive and recording technologies, the automobile has exerted a hypnotic hold on the imaginations of popular songwriters, suggesting that a natural harmony exists between their form of expression and this particular theme.

It is inevitable that any twentieth-century art form should delineate cars to some extent, given their dominion over our everyday lives: what is remarkable about American popular music is the *ubiquity* of the automobile's presence. A study of the course of automobile-related music indicates not only that the car has inspired constant subject matter for aspiring minstrels but that this has remained true even as music and transportation have undergone fundamental transformations. Improved technology revolutionized both music and automobiles in the period immediately following World War II, but they remained steadfast to one another, providing an important voice for a rising generation of Americans eager to leave their impress on the national culture. Specifically, the hybrid strains of rock and roll music depended heavily on the independence offered by racy new automobiles in the early 1950s to sound a barbaric yawp over the rooftops of [jazz musician] Benny Goodman's America. . . .

High-Life Aspirations

The bonanza following World War II made cars universally affordable and fostered dramatic technological improvements that pushed an already car-crazy nation to the brink of lunacy. This mania expressed itself through all the normal media: film, literature, the fine arts, and, of course, music. No genus of popular expression has celebrated the automobile with more feeling and attention to nuance than "rock and roll." The enormous body of music contained within this ill-defined rubric has been intimately connected with the automobile throughout its brief but mercurial history. Rock performers have not only sung the praises of the car but have traditionally dedicated every sequined fiber of their beings to the pursuit of what we might loosely define as an "auto-mobile" existence, something far broader than the general itinerancy required of musicians. In the rock and roll lexicon, cars have evolved beyond simple instruments of transportation to become the very symbols of the high living and conspicuous consumption sought out by artists and savored by the public.

Blues and the Automobile

To fully gauge the extent to which this is true, it is useful to compare rock and roll, which by most accounts emerged in the early 1950s, to the simpler blues music that preceded and fostered it. While many genres of music contributed to the gumbo soup that became rock and roll, the blues was arguably its most immediate ancestor, especially for its emphasis on the individual guitar player. The southern black Americans who created the blues legacy understood all too well the nature of long-distance travel. Many were men who went from town to town on a moment's notice to work an odd job or play a low-paying gig. They did this by riding the rails, hitchhiking, or simply walking along the highway, for theirs was anything but a lucrative calling, and transient, black car-owners were few and far between in the 1930s rural South. . . .

It consequently comes as no surprise that a great many blues songs were about the predicament of the lonely outsider, drifting from place to place. The railroad became a recurring blues motif, strongly evocative of this transiency and the need to escape the confines of an inhospitable society. . . .

Linked to themes of separation and escape, train songs generally suggested the end of relationships, not their beginning, and the railroad's dark power inspired as much despair as admiration.

The highway was also a frequent theme in this music, but only as an ironic commentary, since most blues singers were forced to walk along it, and the overwhelming majority of road songs were written from the pedestrian perspective. One of the most famous of all blues songs, Robert Johnson's "Crossroads" (recorded 27 November 1936), is about the predicament of a black man terrified to be on foot at an unfamiliar highway intersection as the sun is setting.

The automobile was less frequently sung about than the railroad within this musical genre, simply because it embodied a type of unlimited mobility—an *active* as opposed to a *passive* right-of-way—that many American blacks were effectively denied in the South. When it did creep into a songwriter's vocabulary, however, it clearly represented something very different from the anomie linked to train rides and hoboing. As defined in this music, cars were sexy and exciting, one might even say liberating, both for the personal privacy they permitted *and* for the social and financial emancipation they proclaimed. . . .

Postwar Innovations

Following victory in World War II, the United States unconditionally surrendered to automania, even in recently impoverished quarters. The war improved the financial climate for all Americans, including blacks who benefited from the manpower shortage in the industrial North. An astonishing 1.6 million blacks left the South between 1940 and 1950, compared to 350,000 in the previous decade. As had been the case in World War I, many found work in Detroit, but even those who did not migrate gained exposure to the automobile with the widespread rise in the standard of living that followed V-E and V-J days [that is, the end of World War II].

The influx of money not only made the automobile more affordable than ever but allowed new technologies to develop that rendered it all but irresistible to millions of consumers emerging from decades of financial torpor. Simply put, the car was reshaped more dramatically in this brief period than at any time in American history. Wartime technology had led to the discovery of ductile metals that could be coaxed into exciting new shapes and bright colors. Fenders were phased out as cars were lowered, streamlined, and covered with chrome. The 1948 Cadillac inaugurated tapered tailfins in imitation of P-38 Lockheed Lightning fighter planes, and one-piece "panoramic" windshields followed in 1950. The development of the overhead-valve, high-compression engine (1949) vastly improved performance, and soon cars were introduced that depended almost exclusively on "muscle" for their appeal (i.e., the Corvette, 1953).

At the same time, improved electrical ingenuity resulted in superior car radios and dozens of other accessories. The instrument-panel radio had been pioneered by GM in 1935 and had been much improved by elliptical speakers (1940), signal-seeking buttons (1947), foot switches (1950), and "favorite station" buttons (1952). The availability of plastic allowed Chrysler to design a blinking, airplanelike "Jukebox Dashboard" with lots of buttons to satisfy a gimmick-crazed marketplace (its very name hinting at the automotive-musical link). . . .

Freedom and Economic Arrival

Teenagers who were spending their Saturdays fixing up hot rods were eager to absorb the strange new electric sounds coming out of their car radios, for each machine signaled a decisive rupture with older, obsolete models. Suddenly, leisure technology had become universally affordable and comprehensible; taking advantage of it, American youth seized, or rather had thrust upon itself, the cultural means of production. As Tom Wolfe has shown in his essays on the custom-car culture of southern California and stock-car racing in the rural South, the automobile allowed the postwar youth to express himself in ways that no machine had, at least in recent memory. It was hardly accidental that George Barris, the Caravaggio of car customizing, opened his business in 1945, just as millions of battle-weary young Americans needed to shift their attention from the war to less serious matters. As the teenager became a potent economic force, his desires as a consumer were increasingly heeded, and it was to this enormous audience that rock and roll addressed itself. . . .

Seeming to suggest the forbidden mysteries of sexuality, both the new music and the new types of automobiles found easy, if not aggressive, acceptance in the concupiscent universe that was 1950s teenage America. Like jazz (and later, funk), the very words *rock and roll* provoked knowing smiles from those who understood the more organic nature of their original slang meaning. It was inevitable that the automobile, as the symbol of the economic arrival of the previously disenfranchised groups constituting the rock and roll audience, would emerge as a central motif in their new form of musical expression. Automobiles offered an easy escape route from restrictive home environments. Appropriately, many of the earliest rock and roll records were directly linked to the automotive experience.

"Rocket 88"

Although there are earlier uses of the off-color phrase "rock and roll," it is generally conceded that the first song to mix the ingredients of modern rock was a tune called "Rocket 88" recorded in Memphis on 5 March 1951 by Jackie Brenston and the Kings of Rhythm (featuring a very young Ike Turner). A paean to the flashy new Oldsmobile model, the song celebrated little beside the joy of being seen riding around in a souped-up vehicle, but apparently this was enough, for it became a number one hit on the rhythm-and-blues charts. Significantly addressed only to women, it invited the listener to go "sporting" with Brenston all over town, then listed the car features (V-8 motor, convertible top, smart design) that made such an invitation irresistible. The generally salacious feel of the song was heightened by the fuzzy tone of the guitar amplifier, which had fallen out of the band's car (appropriately) on the way to the session and was emitting noise like a wounded B-29 bomber.

Sam Phillips, who produced the session for Chess Records, later pinpointed this moment as the birth of rock and roll, and as the man who launched the careers of Elvis Presley, Jerry Lee Lewis, and Carl Perkins, he was in a good position to know. Little Richard acknowledged that "Rocket 88" served as the inspiration for his "Good Golly Miss Molly." Perhaps even more telling is the fact that a white disc jockey in Chester, Pennsylvania, named Bill Haley liked the song so much that he covered it with his country band, the Saddlemen. This showed the crossover appeal of the song. The electricity of the simultaneous black and white influences, to say nothing of the instruments themselves, would soon allow Haley to emerge as the world's first rock and roll star, although he would not enjoy that distinction for long.

The success of "Rocket 88" launched a spate of inferior imitations, including a follow-up number by Brenston himself called "Real Gone Rocket" (July 1951). Before long, the tiny Chess label alone had recorded Billy Love's "Drop Top" (November 1951), Rosco Gordon's "T-Model Boogie" (4 December 1951), Howlin' Wolf's "Cadillac Daddy" (23 January 1952), Johnny London's "Drivin' Slow" (8 March 1952), and Joe Hill Louis's "Automatic Woman" (9 September 1953), which compared his girlfriend favorably to the new GM transmissions being churned out in Detroit. There seemed to be no limit to the poetic inspiration a musically inclined American youth might draw from the national love affair with the automobile.

Elvis's Pink Cadillac

The most evocative symbol of this rising generation of musical teenagers and their automotive priorities remains Elvis Presley, the self-styled "King of Rock and Roll" (Little Richard briefly contested the title, until it grew evident he held a stronger claim to another royal moniker). Like many of the black musicians he admired and imitated, Presley had grown up desperately poor in Mississippi during the Depression, until his parents had packed all their possessions in a beat-up 1937 Plymouth and driven along Highway 78 from Tupelo to Memphis in September 1948. When he began singing, Presley was driving trucks for the Crown Electric Company, and his lifetime fascination with automobiles paralleled that of an entire underclass for whom more expensive luxuries, such as large houses (although Presley later acquired plenty of those), were simply impossible to fantasize about. While majoring in shop at Humes High School in Memphis, Elvis announced in his yearbook that his highest ambition in life was to become a Tennessee state highway patrolman.

For Presley, the supreme emblem of his liberation from poverty was a pink Cadillac; at first, just the idea of one, and later, when circumstances permitted, the reality. Although his father had scraped together fifty dollars to buy Elvis a 1942 Lincoln Zephyr coupe for his eighteenth birthday in 1953, Elvis, like most Americans, saw the Cadillac as the quintessence of the social acceptability that had thus far eluded him. In one of his earliest recording sessions (February 1955), again with the ubiquitous Sam Phillips, Elvis covered a sexy song called "Baby, Let's Play House" by Arthur "Hardrock" Gunter, which taunts a respectable society girl into remaining with the singer to attend to some neglected domestic chores. Elvis, however, fiddled with the words and substituted "pink Cadillac" for a reference to her religion, and a large measure of the song's excitement derives from the singer's feeling of triumph over a girl rich enough to drive such a highfalutin vehicle. . . .

As Elvis grew richer, automobiles became a type of personal currency for him and purchasing them a peculiar form of economic self-expression. He bought all different types of cars; he bought many of them, and he bought them often. Like [French king] Louis XIV distributing small principalities (this metaphor is inexhaustible), the self-made Sun King offered them freely to his attendants, and these munificent bequests served as informal salaries for his otherwise underpaid minions. There are far too many stories of capricious car purchases during the reign of Elvis to repeat them all here, although my favorite is the night he bought fourteen Cadillacs from a flabbergasted Memphis dealer and offered the last of them to an elderly black woman passing by (perhaps a belated assumption of the debt he owed rhythm-and-blues artists). . . .

Chuck Berry's "Maybellene"

Yet another performer who displayed this obsession with the automobile was a former car thief from St. Louis named Charles Edward Berry. Chuck Berry's first song, "Maybellene" (recorded 21 May 1955), reworked a harmless old country tune called "Ida Red" into a sizzling car chase/romance between the singer in his souped-up V-8 Ford and an idealized woman in an elusive Cadillac (what else?). The song cleverly alternates describing the vehicle and the woman, and before long the one becomes a thinly veiled substitute for the other. It begins with the singer leisurely "motorvating" down the road in his V-8 Ford, then spying Maybellene in a Cadillac Coupe De Ville up ahead of him. They engage in a furious car chase with all sorts of sexual undertones until a providential cloudburst cools down our hero's engine sufficiently that he is able to "catch" her at the top of a hill, ending the drama and the song.

"Maybellene" is exciting not only for its original language (neologisms like motorvate) and its mixture of black and white styles (again, the hallmark of early rock and roll) but also for its openly sexual feel and the populistic triumph of the Ford over the Cadillac. Both rhythmically and thematically, this is a far cry from the blues and its general association of travel with despair and escape. In his recently published autobiography, Berry explained the song "was composed from memories of high school and trying to get girls to ride in my 1934 Ford.". . .

Later songs only strengthened the connection he saw between women and automobiles. "Nadine" (4 January 1964) describes another allegorical chase, this time in pursuit of a girl walking toward a "coffee-colored Cadillac." The choice of this wonderfully evocative color could hardly be chimerical, again the car's identity seems to blend with the woman's. Despite another spirited car race and yelling like a "southern diplomat," he can't catch her this time, largely because she moves through traffic like both "a wayward summer breeze" and "a mounted cavalier." Perhaps the most masterful statement of the car/woman conflation occurs in "No Particular Place to Go" (26 March 1964), in which Berry actually has the girl alongside him in his car but sadly cannot undo her protective safety belt. . . .

Like Elvis, Berry fully lived the automotive life he projected in his "oeuvre." His autobiography is full of automobile references, in 1941, at the age of 14, he bought a 1934 V-8 Ford for $35 ($10 down and $5 a month), the same car that inspired "Maybellene." As one of only two students at his school owning a car, his popularity was increased immeasurably. He went on endless joyrides with other "car-crazy" friends, was incarcerated for car theft during one of them, and immediately bought a shiny Buick upon his release from jail. . . .

Following the Presley and Berry examples, legions of young rockers in the fifties and early sixties incorporated songs about cars into their repertoires. Little Richard aped car slogans by calling his "Long Tall Sally" "built for speed." Bo Diddley not only adopted a rocket-shaped guitar with two fins (the Gibson Flying V) that imitated contemporaneous car styling, but claimed to be a "Roadrunner" (1960), the "fastest in the land." James Brown, who also did time for car theft, surely would have disputed the claim. In "Not Fade Away," Buddy Holly's love was "bigger than a Cadillac." The Ides of March warbled "I'm Your Vehicle, Baby," while the Playmates sang "Beep Beep," about a little Nash Rambler beating a Cadillac in a race. The Beach Boys and Jan and Dean released dozens of songs that made it difficult to imagine how the state of California had ever existed before Henry Ford came along. Furthermore, many groups, ranging from the famous to the mercifully obscure, took their names from some of the more mellifluous car names floating around, including the Imperials, the Eldorados, the Continentals, the Cadillacs, and yes, even the Edsels.

Cars were so popular that even the grisly deaths they caused received thorough, almost loving attention. In 1956, Nervous Norvus scored a moderate hit with his novelty, "Transfusion," in which an injured driver asks for blood by saying "shoot me some juice, Bruce" and "pass the claret, Barrett" over dubbed-in crash sounds. Mark Dinning's "Teen Angel" (1960), Ray Peterson's "Tell Laura I Love Her" (1960), and Jan and Dean's "Dead Man's Curve" (1964) all bespoke the same fascination with death and high-speed car crashes that the italian Futurists had shown at the beginning of the century. While not a rock star, James Dean immediately entered the teenage Valhalla following a fiery exit on the California desert in 1955. Eddie Cochran's death in a car crash in England in 1960 accomplished a similar deification.

Personal Expression

Rock and roll continues to exist and seems to exert an enormous pull on the attentions of adolescents worldwide. It is one of the few art forms that we can call genuinely American in its origin, and the automobile continues to stand out as a pivotal subject, certainly more so than in other types of music. This kinship between theme and form is difficult to explain, but it seems to derive from the fact that both represented a "liberating" principle for the individual, something that has hardly met with resistance in American history. *Automobile*, after all, means "self-moving" in a literal sense, and it is astonishing how many early rockers came from dirt-poor backgrounds, using the music to jack themselves up by their bootstraps. [Poet and essayist Ralph Waldo] Emerson would surely appreciate this latest form of self-reliance; on a different subject, he wrote, "All language is vehicular and transitive."

Both the automobile and popular music profited from postwar technology to offer an unprecedented amount of personal expression, and each emphasized the importance of the *solitary* performer, away from the watchful eyes of parents and neighbors. Like the automobile, the electric guitar allowed the independently inclined from all backgrounds to stand up and take charge of their own destinies, relegating the more communal forms of railroad travel and big-band music to inferior, antiquated roles in the postwar hierarchy of cultural values. Chuck Berry was one of the first popular musicians of the twentieth century to stand up and perform his own material solo before a national audience, and he remains notorious for his dislike of support bands. Elvis, Little Richard, Jerry Lee Lewis, and the other giants of fifties rock were all individual performers as well. At least in the teenage mind, which feeds on autonomy to begin with, this rebellious and discordant music has always existed in perfect harmony with the escapism afforded by the automobile. Few nations have ever needed a mood of carefree independence as America did after twenty years of depression and war, and fewer still ever created one quite so lasting.

Individualism and Transgression in Road Movies

Jack Sargeant and Stephanie Watson

According to Jack Sargeant and Stephanie Watson, the road movie is a unique cinematic genre that borrows themes from American Westerns and youth exploitation (or youthsploitation) films. From the Western, the road movie inherited a sense of perspective. The nation appears in road movies as a vast space that is traversable thanks to the automobile. Movie motorists follow the highways on quests or journeys of personal enlightenment in the same manner that wagon trains in Westerns cross the wilderness in search of a promised land. The travelers in road movies, therefore, take on the mythic stature of the early pioneers—those leaving behind the confines of established civilization in order to live life on their own terms.

Linked to this sense of pioneer spirit is the rebellious outlaw attitude embodied by most road movie heroes. Besides embracing rugged individualism, these characters often desire to live outside of society (usually because they no longer fit in society), and the automobile, according to Sargeant and Watson, becomes their symbol of freedom and unrestricted movement. The authors maintain that this conception of the outlaw hero can be traced to youth culture and juvenile delinquency films of the 1950s, in which anti-authoritarianism and a struggle for independence are common themes.

■

Jack Sargeant and Stephanie Watson, "Looking for Maps: Notes on the Road Movie as Genre," *Lost Highways: An Illustrated History of Road Movies*, edited by Jack Sargeant and Stephanie Watson. New York: Creation Books, 1999. Copyright © 1999 by Jack Sargeant & Stephanie Watson & individual contributors. Reproduced by permission.

Using various mid- to late-twentieth-century road movies to illustrate their points, in the next selection Sargeant and Watson show how the themes borrowed from Westerns and youthsploitation films have played out in this modern genre and how these themes have evolved to keep pace with the changing times. Jack Sargeant is an underground film critic and author. Stephanie Watson was his coeditor for the anthology *Lost Highways: An Illustrated History of Road Movies*, from which this article is taken.

ON THE SURFACE, AND AS AN AMERICAN FILM genre, the road movie finds its roots largely in the classic Western film, and the youthsploitation films which emerged in the post-war boom of the fifties. However, as interpretations of these genres have changed, primarily via re-evaluations of American cultural and social history, so the road movie has emerged as a genre that exists as broadly critical of society and hypothesizes geographical movement as allied to cultural shifts both in America and beyond.

America is the mythical "land of dreams", a nation to which people fled from persecution, poverty and hardship in search of a better life. Modern America was founded by immigrants whose journeys from Europe did not end at the ports of the East Coast but spread across the country, firstly in wagon trains as settlers sought to find a "promised land", but later in cars as people pursued their dreams further west. There have been numerous mass migrations in the history of America, from the south to the north following the dissolution of slavery, the boom in the manufacturing industry and the growth in rural unemployment, from east to west during the gold rush, and again from east to west during the depression. As [author] John Jerome writes: "America is a road epic; we have even developed a body of road art, Huck Finn to *The Grapes Of Wrath* to *Easy Rider*, cutting loose a path to the dream." Fordism led to the ready availability of mass-produced cars that enabled people to transverse the vast distances across the continent. Ultimately, in America, the freedom espoused in the constitution found its realisation within car culture.

New World Heroes

While many who colonized the continent were farmers, establishing small rural communities (beginning with the Puritans and Quakers), it was the pioneering frontiersman who has emerged as the mythic, archetypal American hero. The frontiersman had an intricate relationship with the wilderness, he represented the first movement of European civilization, yet also understood the topographical nature of the landscape, having a relationship to it that was akin to, and informed by, that of the indigenous Native Americans. The mythology of the frontiersman as rugged individualist can be traced to the Old West, with historical figures such as Daniel Boone emerging as the personification of the pioneer spirit. This figure, the lone individual, is not a criminal, but recognizes no legislation other than a combination of the natural laws demanded by survival in the wild and a quasi-Christian sense of moral certainty.

Such mythic figures also exist as separate to the heroes associated with Europe, having evolved to show the new sense of identity that was different from that of the "Old World", which was identified as a zone of constriction, as against the apparent freedom of the continent before them. This notion of a new or "born again" American hero pitted against the moral corruption of Europe, is very potent in American mythology. One of the major characteristics of the American hero is his ability to transform his identity, to become someone else. As the nation aged, this attribute took on a darker side as dream turned into nightmare. The ultimate American paranoiac expression of transformation, as a danger intrinsic to the nation's psyche, appears in the figure of the serial killer whose search for identity through killing others remains undetected within society.

This duality of good/bad power to transform identity was initially reflected in the American hero/anti-hero being pitted against the world around him. The dangers of transformation were seen to come from outside of the American psyche. Writers and filmmakers still generally favoured the "new democratic" American hero against that of the "Old World" aristocratic gentleman hero, whose fixed and hierarchical social status was based on his mythological Greek and Roman predecessors. Failure of the "new democratic" hero was invariably displaced onto some hidden "Old World" corrupt intervention.

In later works, the hero often appeared as an anti-hero pitted against a corrupt and repressive American government, and ultimately society. The figure of the anti-hero is often a version of an earlier hero whose society has abandoned or disillusioned him with its corruptness. The American hero often overlaps with that of the anti-hero because of America's founding status of being a place of non-European beginning yet also trying to define itself against its European roots. This explains the road movie's dual trajectory of offering both escape and/or freedom.

Outlaws

One of the most enduring mythic figures to emerge is that of the outlaw, and especially the lone gunfighter, surviving by a combination of wits and skill; historical figures such as Billy the Kid and Pat Garrett became immortalized within Western films. Such figures are clearly echoed within the protagonists of road movies such as *Easy Rider*, *Vanishing Point* (Richard Sarafian, 1971), or *Drugstore Cowboy* (Gus Van Sant, 1989), all of which feature characters who exist on the fringes of society. The more ruthless—but nevertheless morally certain—gunfighters played by Clint Eastwood in films such as *The Good The Bad And The Ugly* (Sergio Leone, 1966) find their counterparts within characters such as Max in the *Mad Max* trilogy (George Miller, 1979, 1982, 1985), whilst the traveling vampires in *Near Dark* (Kathryn Bigelow, 1987) recall numerous bandits and outlaws from countless Westerns.

The figure of the outlaw/anti-hero—especially in the road movies located within the American south—also emerges as an individualistic hero against a stupid, often comically absurd authority; see for example, the "good outlaws" of *Convoy* (Sam Peckinpah, 1978), or *Smokey And The Bandit* (Hal Needham, 1977) and its numerous sequels. In these films the very titles evoke the colloquialisms of CB Radio, the mode of communication of those in perpetual motion. In these films the character of the Bandit must also be seen as a representation of the mythical untamed Rebel Spirit of the south, unwilling to succumb to the economic dominance of the Union, akin to popular historical folk figures such as Jesse James. An emphasis that was made even stronger in the television series *The Dukes Of Hazard* (Rodney Amateau, William Asher, 1979–1985), whose protagonists drove a car named the General Lee.

The heroines of *Thelma And Louise* (Ridley Scott, 1991) are also "good outlaws", forced by necessity into a cycle of transgressions for which they eventually pay with their lives. The protagonists of road movies are often linked to crime (either they are fallen or about to fall, recalling the Western theme of law/lawlessness), whether as naive criminals on the run such as in *They Live By Night* (Nicholas Ray, 1949), or robbers in *The Getaway* (Sam Peckinpah, 1972). This emphasis recalls the myth that it is possible to escape from the past and start again elsewhere, that roads eventually lead to freedom.

Youth Culture

If it is the Western genre that provides the epic landscapes, the belief in freedom, the search for a better tomorrow, and the outlaw mythology, then the other influence on the road movie is the youth culture and the juvenile delinquency exploitation film. In America owning a car—or even having access to the family car—is a mark of independence, individuality and maturity. With the emergence of youth cultures in the aftermath of the Second World War, the car played a key role, representing an extension of the driver's identity. Cars frequently enable youth to draw a distinction with the conservative adult world of their parents, for whom cars are simply a mode of transportation. In cinema this relationship can be seen in films such as *Rebel Without A Cause* (Nicholas Ray, 1955) and *Hot Rod Rumble* (Leslie Martinson, 1957); (this emphasis on car culture also occurs in the irritating fifties nostalgia movies such as *American Graffiti* [George Lucas, 1973], and *Grease* [Randal Kleiser, 1978]). Many road movies recall this cultural construction of the car as a point of rupture with the recognizably adult world; thus even when protagonists are no longer young, the freedom of transportation enables them to rekindle a youthful spirit. Notably, both *Thelma And Louise* and *Kings Of The Road* (Wim Wenders, 1975) include sequences in which the protagonists find themselves re-living a liberating rebellion, "free" from responsibilities that recalls youth. It is notable that, in the few road movies—frequently comedies—that neither depict youth, nor emphasize a move to a youthful state of mind, the protagonists often experience the road trip with a mixture of confusion, befuddlement, and even fear. In *National Lampoon's Vacation* (Harold Ramis, 1983), *Planes, Trains And Automobiles* (John Hughes, 1987), and *Lost in America* (Albert Brooks, 1985) the middle-aged protagonists are too old, too conservative, and ultimately too scared to undertake the psychic journey that is part of the geographical voyage. It is also notable that in these films the cars are all devoid of the mark of the driver's personality, instead they are stoically practical family vehicles or homogenized, sterile rental cars.

The juvenile delinquency genre can be traced back to the biker movie *The Wild One* (Laszlo Benedek, 1953), and includes such films as *Dragstrip* Girl (Edward L. Cahn, 1957), *Hot Car Girl* (Bernard Kowalski, 1958), and *High School Confidential* (Jack Arnold, 1958), amongst countless others. These films frequently focus on car or motorbike culture, and often locate the protagonists' rebellion, sexual experiences, and dabblings in drink (and sometimes drugs) around cars. Cars also represent the chosen method of confrontation in many juvenile delinquency films; no juvenile delinquency movie is complete without either a race or chicken run sequence, scenes that occur in films ranging from *Rebel Without A Cause* to *Faster, Pussycat! Kill! Kill!* (Russ Meyer, 1966).

The Spiritual Road Trip

However, the youth rebellion against the adult world emerged not just in largely imaginary cinematic representations of flick knives, greasers and chicken runs but also within a wider social context. In Jack Kerouac's beat novel *On The Road* (1957), the hipsters journey across both the country and through their own psyches. The two journeys combine, suggesting that only through experience can one know oneself. In Kerouac's novel, from which—as writer William Burroughs noted—"a whole migrant generation arose", the road trip is as much an internal voyage as an external geographical movement, the inner voyage providing a "new frontier". Kerouac's life was evoked, with questionable success, in John Byrum's *Heart Beat* (1979). Following the beats' journeys youth culture, travel, and expanded consciousness became inexplicably linked within the popular imagination. This link was best illustrated by Ken Kesey and his Merry Pranksters who, in 1964, climbed onto a psychedelic-painted school bus to travel back from the West Coast with the "good" news—and copious quantities of LSD. Whilst Kesey may have been the first, his bus of stoned travellers was not the last; in 1968 the Manson family climbed upon their (ultimately) infamous black bus in order to expand minds and meet similarly disaffected individuals.

The drug culture of the sixties fed into the transgression of boundaries, both physical, social, and personal, which road movies highlight. Drugs offer a collapse of the interior/exterior duality that defines classic constructions of being, allowing and facilitating the expansion of the previously prescribed limits of the psyche, enabling the stoned mind to stretch across the landscape, free from the perceived constraints of the body, just as the body in motion is free from the constraints imposed upon it by the claustrophobia of the city. See, for example, the hallucinatory state of the biker protagonists of *Easy Rider*, actualized in a New Orleans graveyard, but suggested repeatedly by the *mise-en-scène* and stoned rock soundtrack. *Easy Rider* brings together the topographical scale of the Western, the energy of youth rebellion, the post-beat expanded consciousness, with the existential socio-political angst of the times with its now legendary marquee slogan "A man went looking for America and couldn't find it anywhere.". . .

Wandering the Open Road

Roads act as spaces in-between—they transverse apparently empty zones—and the boundaries both geographical and cultural that define social existence in the city or town no longer exist. There are no certainties on the road, only potentialities. Whilst journeys focus toward a final destination, detours are always possible. Other journeys never seek or reach a final destination, becoming extended wanderings with no clear teleological goal. In America's vast landscape, with its frequent seemingly endless straight roads, it is still possible to stray from the path.

The highway represents the circulatory system of the wider zone of the nation state, its routes criss-cross the barren landscape. The highway exists as a line that traces the borders and boundaries of established order, threatening to collapse into anarchy at any moment yet never fully disavowing the presence of civilization. The continual imminence of chaos on the highway becomes the object of terror in texts such as the horror film *Race With The Devil* (Jack Starrett, 1975), the science fiction films *Death Race 2000* (Paul Bartel, 1975) and *Mad Max*, and even the comedy *Planes, Trains And Automobiles*, in which Steve Martin is cast as a bewildered and lost traveller who is forced by the cancellation of his flight to transverse an ultimately alien mid-west by other means. This potential for disaster even on the supposed safety demarcated by the freeway belongs in part to the notion of the wagon trains, which crossed the supposedly uncivilized landscape at continual risk from attacks by native tribes, a myth that informs Westerns such as *The Covered Wagon* (James Cruze, 1923) and *Stagecoach* (John Ford, 1939). . . .

The vision of the open road eternally vanishing into the horizon always promises greater possibilities and journeys to come. Road movies offer audiences a glimpse at an ecstatic freedom. Following the classic Westerns the *mise-en-scène* emphasises the vastness of the terrain, not only locating the individual protagonist's journey within the greater zone of the wilderness, but also allowing the audience the visual pleasure of the spectacle of the landscape, itself a mythical and poetic aspect of the construction of the American identity.

Yet in the genre's emphasis on the spaces between there is a simultaneous acknowledgement of the power of the city. In road movies the city can be both the place from which protagonists flee and/or the final destination. It can represent both the past which must be escaped, as in *Thelma And Louise*, *Wild At Heart* (David Lynch, 1990), and *True Romance* (Tony Scott, 1993), and the holy grail which offers future possibilities as in *Easy Rider*, *Mad Max: Beyond Thunderdome*, and *Kalifornia* (Dominic Sena, 1993). The city itself can represent a microcosm of the larger country, and journeys within the city can become mimetic representations of the larger cross country road trips, with protagonists facing the same dilemmas, questions, and search that happen in the narratives of classic road movies. . . .

The desert, more than any other space within the genre, acts as a symbolic zone in which recognizable signifying practices collapse and identity loses its previous boundaries (for example, Michelangelo Antonioni's *The Passenger*, 1975). It exists as a void in which long-established meanings vanish, the insane heat drives images to haze and nothing is as it once seemed; the sun burns into the retina, human life and the individual subject are always at risk from greater forces and/or the continual threat of pure chaos. Historically the desert is a space in which protagonists are tested and emerge as transformed, in narratives that go back to the Bible, and Jesus' forty days and nights spent in the wilderness. . . .

Modern Odyssey

On the road anything appears possible because nothing seems fixed, the journey itself represents a degree of seduction as the protagonists leave the confines of their world and see the geographical expanse of their future before them. . . . As the past vanishes in the rear view mirror new liaisons are formed and new potentialities emerge. The journey offers the protagonists multiple possibilities, as they either search for a better future or escape the constraints of the past. . . .

The quest drives many protagonists of the road movie, as they travel in search of a better future, a new life, or greater potentialities. The quest theme recalls the original mythic journeys such as that detailed in Homer's *Odyssey*, but its modern form places emphasis on the voyage taken westwards, intrinsic to American history and the western mythology. The notion of the quest also hints at the wider aspects of the genre, in films not immediately associated with the road, yet bearing many of its narrative accoutrements, ranging from Jim Jarmusch's postmodern Western *Dead Man* (1995) and the *Star Trek* television series (1966–1969).

CHAPTER

4

EXAMINING POP CULTURE

Roadside America

The Evolution of America's Gas Stations

John Margolies

The evolution of the gas station in America paralleled the development of the first automobiles. The earliest gas stations were primitive pumping facilities, sometimes no more than a pump handle fastened to a gasoline drum that either sat at a fixed location or was towed on a horse-drawn cart to awaiting customers. As the number of autos and the demand for gas increased, more modern-looking gas stations sprang up at convenient intersections or traffic stops. By the late 1920s the electric gasoline pump with the familiar meter stood outside these establishments, beckoning customers with their lighted domes and shiny metal frames.

As photographer and pop culture lecturer John Margolies outlines in the following article, the gas station's greatest period of evolution occurred between the 1920s and the 1940s. During this time the number of automobiles in the United States increased from 8 million to over 30 million. The increased demand for gasoline prompted the building of more and more gas stations, which in turn fostered greater competition in this crowded marketplace. As Margolies states, the competition motivated gas station owners to provide more services to the motorists, and the simple filling stations gave way to service stations that offered oil lubes and basic car

■

repair. Because of expanded services and the need for repair bays, Margolies explains, the service stations had to adopt new, grander architecture. By the 1930s large, standardized gas stations sponsored by one petroleum company or another were the norm in more heavily trafficked areas. And by the 1940s, with so many full-service stations dotting the landscape, the winners in the battle for customers were the stations with the most creative, idiosyncratic architecture and the friendliest, fastest service.

BY THE ONSET OF THE 1920s, THE AUTOMOTIVE boom was going full blast, created by a fortuitous confluence of circumstances and events. More and better roads, a glut of gasoline on the market (the price fell from about 25 cents a gallon to 18 cents during this decade), and a nearly threefold increase in the number of cars (from about eight million in 1920 to some twenty-three million in 1929) were just some of the factors contributing to American automania.

To fuel this increased mobility, there was an explosion in the number of gas stations built in what were, quite literally, the roaring twenties. In 1921 there were some 12,000 drive-in stations operating; this number leaped to 116,000 by 1927, and 143,000 by 1929. Another staggering statistic about gas station growth is that while in 1919 some 47 percent of the gasoline was sold by grocery stores, general stores, and hardware stores, these outlets had virtually disappeared by the end of the 1920s. In 1929 gas and filling stations were selling 91.7 percent of the gasoline produced.

From Filling Station to Service Station

"Service stations have sprung up like mushrooms in the last few years and many different types have been introduced," states an article from 1922 in Standard Oil Company of Ohio's magazine, which continues, "some in their newness quite attractive, while others apparently expensive, neither practical or pleasing." An issue of Union Oil's magazine from 1923 is more upbeat, at least about its own stations: "The service station of today is, in many cases, a study in architectural beauty . . . we have stations ranging from the small wooden building with pump in front to what is known as the super service station."

In the early 1920s many of the gas outlets were unattractive and not very well equipped, but as the decade progressed stations became more sumptuous and extravagant. They evolved boldly from "filling" to "service" stations, this change being one manifestation of the intense competition among too many retail facilities vying for the same dollars. In 1923, tetraethyl lead was introduced as an antiknocking compound in gasoline, and this caused a proliferation of gas pumps—now, in addition to "regular" there was "premium" or "ethyl." Open or semienclosed grease pits were replaced by hydraulic lifts beginning in 1925. The new equipment was often housed in enclosed service bays attached to stations and sometimes euphemistically dubbed "lubritoriums."

The newer, improved stations of this period, in addition to being larger and more attractive, were also characterized by their larger, landscaped lots, wider driveways, and islands with several pumps, sometimes covered by canopies or freestanding shelters. The buildings themselves were often heated and contained "immaculate" restrooms. By the mid-1920s, the sales of automotive equipment (called TBAs in the trade—an acronym for tires, batteries, and accessories) were being promoted, and sales rooms were added to stations. Later in this decade, equipment to wash cars became part of the package.

Snappy Service

"Free" services were also being expanded and perfected. Cadres of gas station attendants in snazzy uniforms would check the oil, fill radiators, inflate tires, and clean windshields. Commenting on the nature of this service, a Union Oil article explains, "The [best] approach may be summed up in politeness, thoughtfulness, or in any and all of the ramifications of the Golden Rule. . . . In the eyes of the public the operator is the company, and impressions are formed from the treatment received."

Just how hyperextended this notion of "service" had become by the early 1930s can be found in gas station operator Fred Taylor's reply to a survey conducted by Phillips 66. He describes the "Taylor-SERVICE" at his station in Ottawa, Kansas, to which he attributes his increasing sales: "Our explanation for this increase . . . is the unusual 'drive-in' service that other stations in this city do not give. It is a three-man service. Here is how it works: A car drives in on the drive way—we don't wait for him to stop to ask him what he wants—we run out to meet him—. That is to say that all three men meet the car arriving on the drive. One man fills the radiator—another man checks his oil—and shows the driver the oil rod, and the third man fills the tank. After the radiator and oil man get through their job, they wipe the windshield and windows until the third man has made the change and the customer starts his car down the drive way."

All of the service and hoopla culminated in the one-stop superstation of the late 1920s. One huge station in Washington, D.C., was operating with fifty-two pumps. And SOHIO came out with its "English Tudor Hunting Lodge" in Cleveland in 1929—the first of thirty "state of the art" stations to be built. It was an L-shaped building with six service bays, two sales areas, and a women's restroom that rivaled the "lounges" in a movie palace. These one-stop "service centers," open twenty-four hours a day seven days a week, were the ultimate expression of the gas station craze. Not that many were constructed before the grim reality of the Great Depression set in and required at least a little moderation in approach.

Nonetheless, the trend of "super service stations" continued well into the 1930s. More service bays were added to existing stations, portending a growing emphasis on the auto repair business. There was also more attention given to the marketing of automobile-related products—additional display and sales spaces were incorporated in station design, and display areas were made a part of the pump islands.

Architecture

In the fury of the gas station building boom, several architectural types emerged that characterized nearly the entire vocabulary of the genre until its demise. Among these types, several had already begun to appear in the first wave of gas station designs.

The amorphous and architecturally undistinguished little shacks and sheds were a mainstay of the old days. Because of their ad hoc simplicity and inexpensiveness, little buildings such as these have continued to be utilized through the years. Gas stations were, after all, one of the primary small, individually operated businesses. The little guy with only a couple of pumps out front often wanted just a makeshift shelter-station. These dinky creations cropped up nearly everywhere, and some of the more solidly built examples cling to life today across America.

Prefabricated steel buildings, known as "crackerboxes," were first used in the midteens and proliferated by the thousands in the 1920s. They were eminently practical, inexpensive, and very easy to erect, and one source has described them as the "Model T" of gas stations because of their economy, reliability, and durability. Many oil companies used crackerboxes, although the Shell Oil Company's use of them in California may have been their definitive expression. One account from the early 1920s describes how Shell built some one hundred service stations in six weeks along the 260 miles of road between San Jose and Santa Barbara. Each station took only ten days to construct.

Another popular solution for a service station design was to make it look like a little house, proving, once and for all, that a house is not necessarily a home. The house form also helped the station to blend into residential neighborhoods. Two major oil companies, Pure and Phillips, introduced quaint English country cottage–style stations in 1927. Pure Oil introduced its blue-and-white "rain spitter" (so nicknamed because of its steeply pitched blue tile roof) in Indianapolis, complete with window shutters, flower boxes, and a large bay window. The first Phillips cottage opened in Wichita, and by 1930 there were 6,750 of them in twelve states. The Phillips station had a central "chimney" (the Pure model had end chimneys), and each station was painted a distinctive dark green with orange and blue trim to make it stand out from the competition.

While the Pure and Phillips stations utilized traditional architectural styles to establish their identities, just as SOHIO had done with its superstations, many other major oil companies called upon a full range of decorative eclecticism to establish regional and national identities for their building programs. Until World War II, the Gulf Oil Company built in styles suitable to the area where the station was located—colonial in the Northeast and Spanish stucco in Florida and California. The Jenney Oil Company in New England and Standard Oil of New York produced various types of "colonial" visions, while the Ventura Oil Company in Los Angeles opted for a mission-style design.

The final, and by far the most entertaining and intriguing, design type for the gas station was the building in the shape of a recognizable object. Sometimes the shape of the building made sense because of its petroleum imagery. There were gas pump–shaped stations in Maryville, Missouri, and Lancaster, Pennsylvania, and an oil can–shaped station in Buchanan, New York. In the 1920s there was a chain of shell-shaped Shell stations in North Carolina, one of which survived and was placed on the National Register of Historic Places.

Others of these stations made less sense symbolically, although for commercially practical purposes they were definitely hard to miss. There have been iceberg-shaped stations in Ottawa, Kansas, Roanoke, Alabama, and Albuquerque, New Mexico; many a windmill and tepee; and lighthouses galore as recognizable beacons amidst the seas of roadside traffic.

Growth and Competition

Gas stations, great and small, grand and mundane, continued to multiply as the era of the Great Depression loomed. But, concentrating upon the gas station phenomenon alone, one might have logically posed the question "What depression?" The overbuilding of gas stations in the 1920s was exceeded only by the building boom of the 1930s. There were 143,000 retail outlets for gas in 1929, 170,000 by 1933, and this number ballooned to a staggering 231,000 in 1940.

Because there were so many gas stations—it seemed that one cropped up nearly every block or two in an urban area—the competition for customers accelerated. Uniforms and services became more elaborate, advertising campaigns in magazines, newspapers, and on radio became more intense and omnipresent, and promotional giveaways more numerous and lavish.

The new and almost necessary trend in gas station design was not to blend in, but to stick out and demand customer attention. This increased emphasis upon architectural self-expression is echoed in a statement in a 1941 issue of Gulf's *Orange Disc* magazine: "Today the motorist can pass by the unattractive, out-of-date gasoline station and drive on for many miles to an up-to-date, attractive station for the products he needs. One glance at the station will tell him what he may expect. He has learned that the modern station is where he can find the most complete selection of products, the best lubrication and car washing facilities, a complete stock of tires and accessories, and above all the courteous, well-trained attendants who can service his car in the proper manner."

The other major marketing trend that emerged in the 1930s was the so-called trackside operation where gas was dispensed at cut-rate prices on a no-frills basis. Usually the gas was sold from an actual railroad tank car sitting on the tracks, although sometimes the tank cars were moved to tracks beside the road or a building was constructed in the shape of a tank car. But the whole idea of cut-rate, no-frills marketing, which was accompanied by the emergence of private brand companies, which became known as "independents," foreshadowed the coming era of self-service and the eventual decline of the service station itself.

From Idealism to Practicality

The tank car station, real or fabricated, did continue the entertaining trend of bizarre and idiosyncratic service station designs. In what was perhaps the most outstanding example of "Pop" architecture in this era was a lighthouse station built by Gulf at the terminus of the Dade County Causeway in Miami Beach in 1938. An article in Gulf's *Orange Disc* magazine of that year tells us that it was a "beautiful and imposing" building "acclaimed by many as 'the swankiest service station in the world.'"

The advent of World War II marked the end of a grand and glorious era in the history of the gas station. Indeed, it marked the end of an age of idealism and innocence in American culture. Never again would there be the fervor and zeal of the free-enterprise system so sumptuously and joyously expressed in commercial design. The new reality after the war would be more ascetic, economical, and practical, and what little joy remained in the commercial environment would be expressed in scaled-back imitations of the big-time hoopla of the "wonder years" from 1920 to 1940.

The Golden Age of Drive-In Restaurants

Jim Heimann

Although the concept of "curb service" restaurants in America began at the beginning of the twentieth century, drive-in food stands got their jump start in the 1920s when the government kicked off a major road improvement campaign. Some of these 1920s roadside stands offered car service—that is, food brought to the customers' car by carhops—but menus were kept limited to ensure speedy service. Hot sandwiches, coffee, and beer were common fare. In the late 1920s and early 1930s, during the era of Prohibition, roadside restaurants acquired their reputation for serving fountain drinks and milk shakes, and menus expanded. Also in the 1930s, drive-ins developed distinct architectural styles so they would stand out from the growing competition. In the following decade, with the post–World War II building boom, drive-ins flourished as more and more Americans took to the road for work and pleasure.

The drive-in restaurant is perhaps most widely associated with the 1950s and 1960s, as Jim Heimann describes in the following article. Heimann, a graphic artist and educator who has written on pop architecture and regional history, acknowledges that the perceived heyday of the drive-in was a period of great innovation and change. Architectural styles were modernized to include overhangs that afforded car

■

Jim Heimann, *Car Hops and Curb Service: A History of American Drive-In Restaurants, 1920–1960.* San Francisco: Chronicle Books, 1996. Copyright © 1996 by Chronicle Books, LLC, visit ChronicleBooks.com. Reproduced by permission.

customers some protection from the elements, juke-
boxes and other entertainments were provided for the
teenage patrons, and carhop service began to give
way to walk-in dining. However, during this era two
major changes took place that led to the decline of
drive-ins. First, the newly developed interstate highways directed traffic patterns away from the downtown locations where drive-ins had thrived. Also, the
fast-food franchises became extremely popular,
putting most drive-ins out of business. Heimann
laments that by the end of the 1960s most drive-ins
either closed or became fast-food franchises that offered none of the frills or personalized service of the
drive-in dining experience.

THE SLOW DEMISE OF THE DRIVE-IN BEGAN IN A
period that is generally perceived to be its golden age. In the
'50s and '60s the drive-in restaurant was faced with several
challenges that would weaken its position in the food service
industry and eventually place it on an endangered species list.

Still riding a crest of success in the early '50s, drive-ins
were part of a nationwide eating binge that the entire restaurant field profited from. The National Restaurant Association
reported in 1953 that eating out was a $16 billion a year in-
dustry, fueled by an increased population, a shorter work
week, more travel, more suburban restaurants, and, ominously,
a greater demand for take-home food.

Teenagers Invade the Drive-Ins

In the early '50s, families and teens congregated at the drive-
in, which provided an amicable atmosphere for both groups.
The family trade was one segment of the market drive-in owners went out of their way to please and cultivate. Baby bottles
were gladly warmed and the kiddies had their own junior
menus of smaller portions at reduced prices. A dining room, in
conjunction with car service, provided a perfect place for
birthday parties. Youngsters at Hody's Los Angeles drive-in
gobbled up a free, decorated cake. At the end of a drive-in
meal, treats or prizes were handed out by a car hop with a wide

smile and a cheery, "Come back soon!" But, when a carload of teenagers pulled into a drive-in lot they were neither greeted nor sent off in the same manner. They were becoming a stubborn problem.

The Eisenhower era marked a shift in the mood of the country. There were communists, a cold war, and civil rights issues to contend with. There were beatniks and sputniks; there was Marilyn Monroe, Elvis Presley, and rebels without a cause. What used to be a clear-cut, black-and-white world was now an ambiguous gray and a rock 'n' roll pink.

Teenagers, who for the first half of the century had been known as young adults, discovered a niche for themselves in the fast-moving '50s. Their growing ranks as part of the baby boom had advertisers and retailers catering to their needs as never before. Disposable income and increased mobility or "having wheels" moved hangouts from the local soda fountain to the most logical spot: the drive-in. There teens could either be a blessing or a restaurant's downfall. They were often its downfall, because they never left. A business which depended on speedy service and quick turnaround would bottleneck if customers lingered too long. Teens didn't order large meals, yet they could make them last for hours, and they were a potentially volatile bunch. Radios blared and tempers flared. Most of the time, teens weren't welcome. Owners and managers agreed that the teen problem was driving away their most treasured commodity: the family, which avoided the littered lots, the jammed service areas, and the traffic caused by perpetual cruising.

Owners banded together to find solutions for the growing teen dilemma. Some banned teens completely, which was promptly followed by a decrease in revenues. Other tactics included enforcing a minimum order or time limit on lingering. One Lincoln, Nebraska, owner suggested eliminating a tray when serving only coffee or soda so that, "they would move on sooner." A gate system was another solution. It provided tokens to customers who made a minimum purchase; customers returned the token to exit the drive-in's gated lot. If the minimum wasn't met, a token could be purchased for a quarter. Management was careful to point out to regular customers that such a system was installed to improve lot safety and service and to reduce congestion, but the problem persisted. For some teen-agers, drive-ins were the high point of their social lives. For owners, the teenagers were a threat, gradually driving them out of business as family trade dwindled. Owners tried to be sensitive to their future customers and attempted to satisfy both the teenagers and the community, but to no avail. Guards were hired and restaurant associations across the country issued teen disturbance policies. In Pasadena, California, residents of a nearby Bob's Big Boy Drive-In sought a county ordinance banning rowdy behavior surrounding the establishment. Neighbors complained that youths were "using loud and indecent language above blaring car radios. . . . The young people throw their beer cans, bottles and litter in the streets and yards with complete disregard for the residents." The Bob's Big Boy organization solved the problem by eliminating the drive-in facility when they expanded the restaurant. In spite of this growing problem, many drive-ins continued to operate smoothly and concentrate on innovative ways to improve building design and service to continue attracting customers.

Drive-In Design

The modern style of drive-ins introduced in the late '40s continued to exert their influence and proliferate. Tiny Naylor's Drive-In, built in 1949 by Douglas Honnold at the corner of Sunset Boulevard and La Brea Avenue, presaged '50s drive-in design. Taking its cue from the fledgling jet age, the protective canopy overhang, punctured by palms, soared toward the intersection. *Drive-Inn Restaurant and Highway Cafe* magazine declared it, "startling" and "the world's most modern drive-in." Its $200,000 price tag included a mile of fluorescent lighting and three hundred feet of radiant heating pipes buried in the terrazzo sidewalks to keep car hops and customers warm.

A similar design but with less panache was used in 1951 at Merle's Drive-In in Corona Del Mar, California. The marquee-style overhang zipped out to the highway and was supported and pierced at the end by an inverted pylon. The main building was a clipped octagon with front panels forming glass walls anchored by a slump stone base.

Departing from this stylistic direction, but contemporary nonetheless, the Clock Drive-In, at La Tijera and Centinela Avenues in the Los Angeles suburb of Westchester, was a bit more aggressive in its visual approach. Built as a combination coffee shop and drive-in in 1951, it was designed by the firm of Armet & Davis, soon to become the premiere coffee shop designers of the '50s. This was an example of well-placed imagination, creating a double-take newness appropriate for this type of commercial venture. A continuous roofline dropped into the ground and was visually supported at the entrance by a two-story wedge made of red porcelain enamel that served as the advertising pylon. Facing the street, the coffee shop was a low-slung horizontal box, its facade a wall of plate glass broken by triangular struts. Located behind the coffee shop, drive-in service facilities received a less dramatic treatment.

While several combination drive-in coffee shops successfully applied this architectural style, such as the Wich Stand in Los Angeles, the self-contained coffee shop made the best use of this imagery, developing a whole catalogue of distinctive buildings and forming a separate architectural genre soon to be coined Googie.

On the East Coast, another drive-in style made its debut in the '50s. The Virginia Gentleman Drive-In in Front Royal, Virginia, by architect Earl R. MacDonald, the Park and Eat in Gulfport, Mississippi, and various Richard's Drive-Ins throughout the eastern seaboard all featured a bare-to-the-bones, two-story industrial hangar structure. An enormous flat roof supported by a glass box held a coffee shop with car service surrounding the building in an oversized lot. Underneath the overhang, banks of fluorescent lights illuminated outside and in, while on top of the roof, free-standing signage announced the restaurant's name. The entire effect was LARGE, but when translated to a smaller scale, this design proved to be a great model for dozens of ice cream stands and burger bars across the country.

Innovations

The extended canopy, introduced by the Pig Stand in 1931, was one more instance of drive-ins melding function and style. Initially made out of canvas, they were used primarily to shield customers from the weather. They later developed into architectural elements functioning in the same way overhangs did. Their

The design and flare of the drive-in restaurants during the 1950s and 1960s offered patrons a fun and entertaining dining experience.

basic shape was usually straightforward and functionally flat, but as their importance to the style of the building increased, a variety of undulating "rock 'n' roll," gull-wing, and multicolored versions appeared. In some instances, the extended canopies could dominate a building, eventually becoming the building itself. In these cases, a clever name like Carporteria Drive-In might be used. At the Drive-O-Matic Drive-In in Hammond, Indiana, a sixty-two-foot conveyor belt ran the length of the aisle beneath the canopy, delivering food on top and returning soiled dishes below. Touted as a labor-saving device, it was one of a long line of ideas developed in the '50s to meet the drive-in's never-ending quest for speed, efficiency, and cleanliness. Fast food service would result from this kind of experimentation. Costly overhead brought on by labor, lease, building, equipment, and food prices prompted drive-in owners to trim any or several of these factors whenever possible.

Take-home service was an effort in this direction. A convenient sideline to curb service, take-out was a courtesy rather than policy for most drive-ins and at first it was slow to catch on. It was the elimination of the car hop that finally made self service a widespread reality. In 1948, two drive-in owners, brothers Richard and Maurice McDonald, did just that. Having run a small orange juice and hot dog stand since 1937 in Arcadia, just east of downtown Los Angeles, they moved farther east to 1398 North E Street in San Bernadino, where they opened an expanded drive-in with car hops. The brothers had the same problem many drive-in owners after the war had complained of—employees that were unreliable and of dubious character. So the McDonalds decided to drop car service and concentrate on a specific menu of ten items that a customer would have to get out of his car to buy. A production line preparing the reasonably priced ten-cent burgers, fifteen-cent French fries and twenty-cent malts was installed, with paper replacing dishes and fingers replacing silverware. The meal was bagged in a speedy twenty seconds. Their 192-square-foot octagonal building was slightly remodeled for the carry-out service, with warming lamps placed above the service windows for chilly nights. Initially customers found the familiar drive-in form confusing without the trademark car hop, but once they became accustomed to walking up and either eating at the counter ledge or in their car, they flooded the place. A 1952 article in *Restaurant Management* featured the McDonald's outlet, running this headline, "One Million Hamburgers and 160 Tons of French Fries a Year." Franchising followed and a few years later a milkshake machine salesman named Ray Kroc became the McDonald's agent, taking the franchise nationwide. A building with comfortable drive-in imagery was sketched by Richard McDonald and realized by local architect Stanley Meston, and the golden arches made their debut in Phoenix, Arizona, in May 1953. The end of the traditional drive-in was fast approaching.

With the climate ripe for this type of service, hundreds of variations of the McDonald's theme began to appear in the early part of the '50s. There was Pay-N-Tak, Thrift-O-Mat, Hamburger Hand-Out, Burger Queen, and the Cheese Hut. All would later be joined by franchises and other fast food outlets by the score.

Along this line of abbreviated service concepts, a Big Boy

(no relation to the Bob's Big Boy chain) Drive-In in Billings, Montana, and the Tastee In and Out in Lincoln, Nebraska, installed microphones along their driveways leading to their small, main buildings. After ordering, customers drove the short distance and picked up their drive-thru meal.

In Florida, Burger King replicated the McDonald's idea with eighteen-cent burgers, walk-up service, and their miracle "Insta" machines for making mass-produced malts and burgers. In spite of these developments, traditional drive-in service managed to hold its own. Big chains helped the industry stabilize and Bob's Big Boy, Steak 'N Shake, Sonic, Dog 'N Suds, A&W and others continued to be successful car hop operations. They were joined by the independently owned outlets spread out in every town and along every highway. Some of these drive-ins could be counted on to provide interesting additions to regular dining fare, all in an attempt to drum up business.

Entertainment

Several drive-ins provided entertainment to go along with the meal. Al and Violet Travelstead at their Howdy Pardner Drive-In in Boise, Idaho, transformed the roof of their elongated carport into a stage, complete with piano, for their mid-week floor shows. Created by the owners, their "Stage in the Air" welcomed local talent while car hops clad in cowgirl garb served the audience in their cars below. Strictly a family affair, the Travelsteads even concocted special fountain items for the tikes—the Little Pedro Parfait and the Mule Train Maverick sundae.

The Snak Shak Drive-In in Chambersburg, Pennsylvania, invited customers to pass the time at their establishment by playing shuffleboard or dancing on the cement slabs that flanked either side of the main building. This summer-only attraction, included a small shed that housed a jukebox and a pinball machine. With these additional diversions receipts doubled. Owner Clara Snyder said, "It certainly has been a real hypodermic for our business.". . .

The Little Chef Drive-In in Louisville, Kentucky, claimed that the new electronic opiate, television, was affecting customer sales because patrons were staying glued to the tube and off of the road. Their response was to buy a fleet of trucks as a sideline to their car service and offer housebound viewers home delivery from their menu. By 1955, these mobile kitchens accounted for 60 percent of the restaurant's business.

In warmer climates where heat was a problem, owners anxious to make customers comfortable in their cars introduced individual air-conditioning units. A hose dropped from a unit attached to the overhang and was inserted by the car hop as the menu was given. Two drive-ins that tried it, the Blue Onion in Las Vegas and Stuart's Drive-In in Houston, reported success, but the idea faded due to the expense, maintenance, and the short season the air conditioner was used. Conversely, in colder climes, heating units were installed beneath overhangs on poles in an attempt to prolong the selling season.

Electronic ordering equipment flourished briefly in the '50s. A few drive-ins had experimented earlier with walkie-talkies, but most restaurants installed the "electronic car hop," promoted by various companies under names such as Servus-Fone, Teletray, and Orda-Phone. A speaker, similar to the kinds used in drive-in theaters, was mounted on a serving station equipped with a permanent menu and tray table. After pressing a button, a switchboard operator would take the order. The press of another button switched on hi-fi music that entertained the customer until meal and bill arrived via car hop. When the patron was ready to go, the tray was returned to the service table and the customer was off.

The Demise of the Drive-In

Several food items introduced in the drive-in at about the same time became so popular they warranted their own separate eating venues. These food outlets added to the growing competition for the drive-in dollar. The pizza craze of the late '50s was emblematic of this trend. Pizza parlors joined a crowded market that included pancake houses, donut shops, and steak joints, making it clear that a culinary shoving match was in progress.

The drive-in restaurant, in transition as the '50s closed, was breathing its last gasp by the mid-'60s. Though portrayed in the media as a thriving teen haven, the drive-in was dwindling. The collective problems and developments of the previous fifteen years were now challenging its very existence. In Southern California, the drive-in had flourished for four decades, but an ever-expanding population was forcing land values up, making most of the prime drive-in locations economically unfeasible. Compounding the problem was the highly developed freeway system, which drained the main thoroughfares of their vitality. Other parts of the country wrestled with similar problems. Ultimately the power of the family dollar determined the fate of the drive-in, and fast food outlets won decisively.

One by one, drive-ins switched over to take-home, self-service, or fast food operations . . . or simply fell into oblivion. The term drive-in now came to mean any restaurant that accommodated a car, but not necessarily service in your car. In the '70s some traditional drive-ins, complete with car hops, dotted the country, but they had become antiquated versions of their former selves. Several chains maintained their car service. Notable were A&W and the Sonic Drive-Ins, which survived the fast food frenzy mainly because of their small-town locations. The independently owned drive-in took a beating from prohibitive start-up and operating costs which left the majority of casual-dining restaurants in the hands of large businesses and corporations. Public indifference and the shifting cultural values evident in the late '60s were also to blame and nailed the drive-in's coffin shut. In 1984, Tiny Naylor's, which had stood at the same Hollywood intersection for thirty-five years, met the wrecking ball. Attempts by preservationists to save the structure were in vain, and in its place a multiunit, nondescript mini mall was constructed. Its destruction was the symbolic internment of a cultural phenomenon fostered in a city consecrated to the car.

Tourist Attractions Along Route 66

Michael Karl Witzel

Known as the Mother Road and the Main Street of America, Route 66 stretches from Chicago to Los Angeles and passes through eight states. From the 1920s until the 1960s this vast roadway was the principle artery of cross-country travel in America. Route 66 provided a steady stream of tourists and travelers to the many cities and hamlets that dotted its path.

 In the following excerpt from his book on Route 66, pop culture historian Michael Karl Witzel describes the unique roadside culture that sprang up along the highway. Motels, gas stations, diners, and tourist traps profited from the flow of travelers' dollars, but as Witzel points out, competition was fierce. The growing number of businesses along Route 66 each sought to stand out from the crowd. Large, colorful signs broadcast the amenities available at motels and gas stations. Sombrero-shaped diners and brightly lit drive-ins offering fountain drinks and hamburgers gave passing motorists a reason to stop. And souvenir shops advertising genuine Indian-made trinkets lured those who wanted to nab a piece of handcrafted Americana. As Witzel asserts, the multitude of these fun and fascinating stopovers eventually made the route itself a tourist destination, not just a means of reaching one. And to Witzel and other road romantics, nostalgia thankfully has kept Route 66 a tourist attraction even after the network of interstate highways that arose in the 1950s made the original single ribbon of pavement obsolete.

■

Michael Karl Witzel, *Route 66 Remembered*. Osceola, WI: MBI Publishing Company, 1996. Copyright © 1996 by Michael Karl Witzel. All rights reserved. Reproduced by permission.

THROUGHOUT THE ROARING TWENTIES AND straight on up to the 1960s, the roadsides along Route 66 jumped with an eclectic mix of attractions. Back then, America's Main Street was the nation's premier ride—a two-lane roller coaster of thrills that rambled through eight states and three time zones. All along the miles of the "linear midway," a diversity of car commerce combined services motorists required with the entertainment they desired.

With a full tank of fuel, a good night's snooze, and a belly filled with road food—motorized attendees of the roadside carnival pushed down on the accelerator to bring on the wonders. Near the highway's western limit in the city of Los Angeles, wheeling past a barbecue stand constructed like an immense pig was an everyday occurrence. Out there, short-order food shacks were shaped like giant toads and juice joints bloated up as oversized oranges.

At the outskirts of town where traffic dwindled, automobile ownership allowed day-trippers to experience the full glory of 66. Beneath the gaping grin of a life-size dinosaur, couples could picnic without care. When a long day of explorations were concluded, it was all the rage to catch 40 winks inside an Indian wigwam, refill one's gas tank at a petrified-wood service station, or dine on a corned-beef sandwich inside the penthouse of a gigantic shoe. Route 66 held an endless array of surprises!

Luring Motorists

With turning a profit of paramount importance, the roadside businesses lining the highway employed every trick they could think of to lure motorists. They had no alternative: When automobile ownership during the teens and 1920s rose to become secondary only to shelter and clothing—the trading climate along America's roadsides became increasingly competitive. As a steady influx of new drivers turned a dirt artery into a transcontinental corridor, new types of industries emerged to accommodate the flow.

Before too long, services that catered to the motor vehicle were duplicated in vast numbers. With the corresponding rise in Route 66 advertisers vying for attention, the raft of billboards and snipe signs common to early motor trails became impotent. At what used to be a quiet country crossroads, Chuck's Chicken Shack now had to contend with a self-contained dining car across the street and a cafeteria on the corner. As travelers sped past with no end in sight, the friendly neighborhood filling station suddenly found itself in competition with two additional "service" stations and a lubritorium on the very same block!

The need to achieve greater visibility—and a unique hook —increased. To break through the visual cacophony, some Route 66 entrepreneurs decided to erect bigger and more brightly lit signs. Others took the craft of outdoor advertising to a new level with neon-lit creations of pressed steel and glass tubing. Born of the merchant's imagination, roadside statues made of plaster and lath were used to attract the motorist's ever-decreasing attention. A few businesses that depended directly on the car for business decided to blend both their building and billboard by utilizing the "programmatic" themes so popular on the coast. By copying the whimsical forms of animals or objects and incorporating them into their buildings, operators blended billboards with architecture. By the time construction crews were laying concrete along the final miles of Highway 66, an exciting roster of restaurants, gas stations, tourist courts, souvenir stands, and other recreational hideaways were entertaining the travelers with architectural theatrics. In Oklahoma, a smiling blue whale splashed about in the waters near Catoosa. Just down the highway in Foyil, tourists were allowed to explore the inside of a multicolored totem pole. Meanwhile, the good folks in Texas slapped an oversized set of longhorns and a ten-gallon hat on just about everything. New Mexico traders adopted the Indian mystique, and in the stretch of road through Arizona the shapely saguaro became a predominant theme. By the time man orbited the Earth, Paul Bunyan had donned a space helmet (with hand-held missile) near Wilmington, Illinois!

Route 66: A Destination in Itself

As the rush to motorize changed America, the "Mother Road" became a bona fide destination in itself. Timid automobile owners who never dreamed of leaving the confines of their state took to the highway with great zeal—just to see how easy it was to travel long distances. Suddenly, the owners of road-side businesses began to realize that there was much more to making money along a busy thoroughfare than just renting out tourist cabins, pumping gas, or serving chili: When a traveler's needs were taken care of and they were ready to continue the journey, thoughts often turned to mementos of the trip. Everyone, it seemed, wanted a souvenir to show the folks back home—proof of exactly where they had been and the adventures they had experienced.

Unprepared for the rising demand, Route 66 operators learned first hand of the motorist's sentimental acquisitiveness: day in and day out, ash trays, towels, tableware, napkin holders, coffee cups, salt and pepper shakers, and anything else that could be carried off began to disappear. In an effort to discourage this depletion of operating equipment and to increase revenue, the idea of selling specialized souvenirs was seriously considered. Unsure of the territory, the trio of roadside services known as gas, food, and lodging were entering the retail world.

At the wayside cafes, cashier stations doubled as display areas for knick-knacks. Colorful matchbooks emblazoned with whimsical captions, cartoons, and other advertisements became the staple item to give away free (when one purchased a cigar or pack of cigarettes). At dining tables, some restaurants slipped imprinted placemats under the table-settings. Featuring facts and figures pertinent to the local area along with idealized reviews of the highway's attractions, they were inexpensive give-aways to keep on hand. Of course, nothing reminded one of eating out away from home as much as a souvenir menu. Statues were cast, coins minted, glassware etched, and guidebooks printed.

For the majority of Route 66 operators, the linen picture postcard became the most cost-effective method to advertise a roadside business and get name recognition on a national level. When it was provided gratis, enthusiastic patrons were more than willing to provide the penny postage and to mail it off—sending home what amounted to nothing more than a personalized, direct-mailer to receptive friends and family. No amount of advertising could equal the hand-written testimonials describing attractions found along the "Great Diagonal Highway."

As pictures were examined on front porches in small-town

America, kids marveled at the sight of their own road vanishing into the distance—tied like a string to a world of possibilities yet undiscovered. It was a world of travel that was opening up to all: In the decade following World War II, the suspension of all gasoline rationing and the production of bigger, better motorcars equated to a renewed level of mobility. Young dreamers who did without were now coming of age and taking to the highways to make their own memories. Highway volume increased so much that by the close of the 1940s, the demand for sentimental sundries spurred a handful of hopefuls in Arizona and New Mexico to jump in with full-scale retail operations.

Trading Posts

Before tourists could hide their wallets, savvy salesmen were recruiting the local Indian crafts people and scouring trade shows for desirable products. Itching to cash in on the coast-to-coast commuter, elaborate merchandising markets—or "trading posts" as they were called—were established at various points along Highway 66. The outskirts of major population centers in the Southwest got more than their fair share, followed by adjoining states and other regions in the Ozarks. In the postwar era, taking a trip down the Will Rogers Highway meant trading with the Indians.

For the vacationing family motoring out to view the wonder of the Painted Desert, trading posts were found to exhibit even more color. The fierce competition for customers ignited an endless duel to install the most saturated neon sign, construct the most colossal fantasy figure, or splash exteriors with the most garish paints. In most instances, all of the outside walls facing the highway became the canvas for a visual sales spiel. Three-foot-high lettering trumpeted an outfit's name as hanging sign boards (edged in jagged cuts) announced the collection of goods inside.

While the visual pulling power of the Geronimo trader had most of the nearby setups licked, one local competitor came up with a way to influence the customer hundreds of miles before they even crossed into the Grand Canyon State. James Taylor, operator of the Jackrabbit Trading Post, joined forces with Wayne Troutner (legendary owner of Winslow's

Store for Men) and traveled Highway 66 on an all-out mission to advertise. Armed with a truckload of signs—bright yellow Jackrabbit signs—he plastered as much of the American roadside as possible with his namesake!

It was a hands-on approach to advertising that over the years fired up motorists' imaginations and developed an invaluable aura of mystery for his merchandising market. At the same time, it heightened the Jackrabbit's status as a Route 66 legend—fueling the interest of vacationers willing to go out and find it. One way or another, cars would eventually drive up to the Jackrabbit Trading Post. Painted in bold letters on a yellow slat billboard, a final exclamation greeted sojourners with a pithy "Here It Is." Perched atop the sign, a silhouette of an immense jackrabbit and a row of companion bunnies caught the eye of passing traffic. Of course, the three-foot-high composition jackrabbit (with yellow eyes) positioned at the front gate didn't hurt business. That was the real magnet for the kids.

In addition to memorable mascots and searing color schemes, most of the souvenir supershops borrowed extensively from Native American heritage. The connection became most obvious in their practical architecture: Influenced by the Iroquois style long house and the rectangular motifs of the Hopi pueblo, trading posts were typically long, low, flat-roofed structures constructed of cinder-block walls and finished in stucco. Ornamentation and decoration were kept to a bare minimum.

Ten miles west of Winslow, Arizona, Ray Meany's fabulous Hopi House set the standard for architectural aesthetics. Made of adobe set in mud mortar, it was a design that featured exposed roof timbers, an exterior staircase, and a restrained application of flamboyant advertising. With most of the tourist markets along Highway 66 designed for maximum flash, Meany's multi-level trading complex was a tasteful exception to the rule.

Indian Goods

Despite the rare operators who showed restraint, showmanship ruled the road: At Winslow's Big Indian Trading Post, a three-story representation of an angry, tomahawk wielding chief (sporting a feathered headdress and a full complement of war paint) nonchalantly rested his arm on a rooftop sign. Tepee Curios in Tucumcari, New Mexico, grafted one-half of a Plains Indian dwelling (outlined with neon tubing) onto its streetside facade. Car customers attracted by the curious sight entered through the pulled-back flap that led them to a standard-sized door opening.

In Lupton, the Tomahawk Trading Post billed itself as the last stop out of Arizona and took Indian weaponry to the extreme. In the parking lot, a massive sign depicting an idealized tomahawk loomed high above multiple lanes of gas pumps. In the "stone" portion of the giant ax, numerals were posted to alert all those zooming past of discount gasoline sold at "truckers' prices."

Inside the trading posts, the atmosphere often matched the excitement of the exterior. Everything under the desert sun was available for purchase. Jewelry was a mainstay, including handmade designs from Navajo and Zuni craftsmen. One could purchase elaborate squash-blossom necklaces, earrings, bracelets, strings of beads, belt-buckles—anything and everything that could hold a chunk of polished turquoise. The Big Arrow trading post in Houck, Arizona, even featured a line of "Squaw Dress Originals by Arlene!"

For the discriminating consumer, there were woven Indian blankets and rugs, tom-toms, belts, purses, and the ubiquitous genuine leather moccasins. For those restricted by budget, miniature cacti, saguaro preserves, and chunks of petrified wood provided shopping satisfaction. Even the children were accommodated with an assortment that rivaled the most modern toy store. Aisles stocked to the brim with tin toys, reproduction bow and arrow sets, cowboy clothes, six-shooter cap guns, wind-up drummers, feathered headbands, and articulated wood rattlesnakes were the reasons kids in the backseat begged their parents to stop!

Sometimes, the parents needed no prodding when it came to visiting the tourist traps—especially if they were the type that offered up real live Indian shows. In that department, the Cliff Dwellings Trading Post near Lookout Point, New Mexico, was one of the Route 66 favorites. There, a half-dozen authentic Indian dancers performed ceremonial routines inside a rustic stockade. Every half-hour, patrons scurried to the rear of the store to be dazzled by a boisterous demonstration of native culture. For the 1950s family trekking their way across the continent there was always ample time left in the itinerary to watch the ceremonial moves of indigenous Americans.

Unfortunately, the live Indian gala proved to be a little too disruptive for sales. While a great gimmick to pull in the crowds, it appeared that many visitors were only there to see the complimentary show. A more suitable equilibrium was attained by the trading posts when native silversmiths, rug makers, and basket weavers were hired to perform their work on site. As visitors watched skilled artisans creating the articles sold, it instilled a marked sense of value into the handmade merchandise. It was a great method of in-store promotion, since customers could be entertained as their sales resistance was being worn down. In the end, moving souvenirs—and truckloads of them—was the primary intention of the traders doing business along Route 66.

Beasts Boost Business

With that goal at the forefront, there was no limit to what the roadside tourist traps would do to boost business. In the Southwestern United States—where the nervous automobile traveler feared the desert and the creatures that lived there—this fact forged an unholy alliance between the highway retailer and the reptile world. By the mid-1950s, the combination curio shop and animal farm had evolved into a hybrid business that guaranteed visitors. Its drawing card? One of the most controversial highway hypes devised by man: the snake-pit!

For farm-raised midwesterners, travelers from the East, and folks who just plain didn't get out much, nothing back home could compare to "Reptile Gardens," the ultimate trading post and slither house located in Bluewater, New Mexico. Billed as the "largest rattlesnake trading post" along the entire length of 66, it housed under one roof all the cold-blooded creatures that anyone would ever want to view during an entire lifetime!

Leading the exotic entourage, a King Cobra 15 feet long occupied the center ring, accompanied by an immense python weighing in at a whopping 200 pounds! As side-show filler, an amazing assortment of cobras imported from India, Malaysia, and Sumatra were put on public display. Crowds marveled at the sight of a Green Mamba, a hideous Gila monster, and dozens of fresh, squirming rattlesnakes! As a matter of course, most tourists checked their shopping bags for stowaways upon departure.

From Mystique to Hokum

Unfortunately, the appeal of the snake shows wasn't enough to sustain the merchants when the Great Highway fell from prominence. With a growing addiction to shopping malls, franchised hamburger stands, thematic amusement parks, video games, and cruise control, the modern motorist began to view the quirky wayside attractions of yesterday's roadways as so much hokum. As vacationers' focus on destinations increased, interest in trading posts and other homespun attractions diminished. As the headlong rush to "get there" edged out simple enjoyment of the motor trip, the sights found along the way became a moot point.

At the same time, the concept of "entertainment" was being redefined by the flicker of images on a cathode-ray picture tube. Television had arrived with a vengeance, embracing the western myth with such vigor that within a few short years, the "home where the buffalo roam" had been relieved of its mystique. Jaded by the endless shows, the sophisticated tourist was more concerned about whether the motel room off the next exit ramp came equipped with a television set rather than real hickory furniture.

As the high-speed interstates sucked the lifeblood from Route 66, the once bustling ribbon of road became nothing more than the molted skin of a bygone era. By the 1970s, the countrywide implementation (and completion) of the freeways instigated by the Interstate Highway Act of 1956 brought an end to the merchandising mania of the old road. In small towns, Wal-Mart discounters usurped the obligations of the curio shops. Along the impersonal miles of the interstate, sprawling truck stops and feeding facilities assumed the responsibility of trading trinkets. Real leather products were now "crafted" in China from genuine imitation vinyl, turquoise stone became colored plastic, and the only reptiles were either flattened on the freeway or made of rubber.

Today, only a few of the tourist traps remain along the road-less-traveled. Most of the extravagant operations have long since gone out of business, their original owners retired, deceased, or disinterested. Other outfits have evolved with the times, but remain mere shadows of what they used to be. While some of the trading post structures have found new uses, the majority have been abandoned. For the adventurous motorist who steers clear of the superhighway in deference to the free road, only crumbling walls, faded murals, and fragments of neon remain as evidence of the way Americans used to get their kicks . . . on Route 66.

Books

Douglas Brinkley, *Wheels for the World: Henry Ford, His Company, and a Century of Progress, 1903–2003*. New York: Viking, 2003.
> Written for the Ford centennial, Brinkley's huge tome may be intimidating, but its wealth of information is unprecedented. The Ford Motor Company opened its archives of documents to the author, who did not hesitate to incorporate the majority into this work. While detailing the history of the company over the past hundred years, Brinkley notes how the specter of Henry Ford and his philosophies have cast a shadow over each stage of the industry's development.

Frank Coffey and Joseph Layden, *America on Wheels: The First 100 Years: 1896–1996*. Los Angeles: General Publishing Group, 1996.
> Perhaps the best recent single-volume overview of automotive history, Coffey and Layden's book was written as a companion to a PBS documentary on cars in America. It is filled with interesting insider quotes and a wealth of photographs and advertisements that bring the narrative to life.

Christopher Finch, *Highways to Heaven: The Auto Biography of America*. New York: HarperCollins, 1992.
> This overview of car culture in America is an excellent resource because of the broad range of topics it covers. While tracing the automobile's history, Finch discusses how cars progressively changed America into an automotive society. He devotes entire chapters to subjects such as the rise of the major automakers, the effects of rapid highway construction on the country, and the retooling of the industry in the face of rising gas prices in the 1970s.

James J. Flink, *The Automobile Age*. Cambridge: Massachusetts Institute of Technology Press, 1988.
> Expanding on a previous volume of automotive history (see next entry), Flink traces the history of the automobile from its inception in Europe to its place of dominance in America. Flink shows how the car impacted such things as labor-industrial relations,

government planning and spending, and the way in which Americans lived out the dream of the good life.

James J. Flink, *The Car Culture*. Cambridge: Massachusetts Institute of Technology Press, 1975.

An automotive historian and social critic, Flink discusses how the automobile industry (and its product) came to define how Americans live. Flink focuses on such luminaries as Henry Ford, Walter P. Chrysler, and General Motors founder Billy Durant, and the way in which their vision of automobile supremacy resulted in tying the health of the national economy to car manufacturing and creating a culture that hungered for automotive advancement without regard for the consequences to society.

Mark S. Foster, *A Nation on Wheels: The Automobile Culture in America Since 1945*. Belmont, CA: Wadsworth, 2002.

Foster, a history professor, begins with the postwar auto boom and follows the impact of the expanding car culture on various aspects of American society. In his brief overview Foster examines such topics as the role of automobiles in youth culture, the rise of suburbia, and the advent of roadside commercial industries.

David Gartman, *Auto Opium: A Social History of American Automobile Design*. New York: Routledge, 1994.

This interesting volume examines the aesthetics of car manufacturing and the way in which even the earliest carmakers had to contend with the outward design of automobiles. Gartman maintains that the look and shape of cars had (and still has) much to do with the requirements of mass production and the efficient running of auto plants.

Owen D. Gutfreund, *20th-Century Sprawl: Highways and the Reshaping of the American Landscape*. New York: Oxford University Press, 2004.

Gutfreund uses case studies to show how suburban sprawl has contributed to urban decay in many major U.S. cities. He maintains that the U.S. government—influenced by the auto industry—has contributed to this sprawl by subsidizing road networks. He also argues that once these road networks were built, the federal government left the maintenance bills to the already overburdened city governments, effectively worsening the state of inner cities and prompting more migration.

Jane Holtz Kay, *Asphalt Nation: How the Automobile Took over America, and How We Can Take It Back.* New York: Crown, 1997.
  Kay, an architecture journalist, launches a thorough critique of the impact of the automobile on America. She blames the car culture for ruining urban landscapes, widening class and racial divisions, and exacerbating a host of health problems that have blighted the nation and society. Incorporating the thoughts of many progressive urban planners and social critics, Kay calls for a rethinking of the relationship between cars and people. This, she hopes, will inspire the kind of activism needed to compel better urban planning and right other wrongs brought on by an automobile-focused society.

David A. Kirsch, *The Electric Vehicle and the Burden of History.* New Brunswick, NJ: Rutgers University Press, 2000.
  While much of automotive history has been defined by the needs of the gasoline-powered vehicle, Kirsch examines how and why electric cars have been shunted to near irrelevance. After laying out the history of battery-driven automobiles, Kirsch moves on to explore the factors that led car manufacturers and society to embrace the internal combustion engine at the expense of electric technologies. He explains, though, that changing social concerns—such as the exhaustion of fossil fuels and environmental considerations—may alter the way motorists think about transportation in the future.

James Howard Kunstler, *The Geography of Nowhere: The Rise and Decline of America's Man-Made Landscape.* New York: Touchstone, 1993.
  A novelist and reporter, Kunstler argues that American communities have been suffering decline for several decades. Poor urban planning has left inner-city neighborhoods blighted, while suburban regions have drifted into a nondistinctive wasteland dominated by shopping malls. Within this larger critique of America's transformation, Kunstler suggests that the automobile has been a significant agent in society's decline. He cites the rampant paving of America and the focus on strip mall communities as evidence that most places in the country are becoming more and more like no place in particular.

Brian Laban, *Cars: The Early Years.* Koln, Germany: Konemann, 2000.
  Using photographs from the Hulton Getty collection, this pictorial treatment of early automobiles is eye-catching. While the images are of prime importance, a textual history (in both English

and German) of autos from the early twentieth century through the 1950s is provided.

Micheline Maynard, *The End of Detroit: How the Big Three Lost Their Grip on the American Car Market*. New York: Currency/Doubleday, 2003.

Noting that domestic car sales in America have declined since the mid–twentieth century, Maynard argues that foreign car manufacturers—primarily the Japanese—have used unique strategies to break the U.S. market. Not willing to take on Detroit in every market, these foreign corporations have targeted small segments of American consumers and eventually eroded domestic sales bit by bit.

Daniel Miller, ed., *Car Cultures*. New York: Berg, 2001.

This unique anthropological study includes chapters concerning how cars and people interact in various cultures of the world. Authors in this collection examine the human attributes afforded to vehicles in many cultures, how vehicles have culturally specific uses beyond mere transportation, and what cars say about class and social status in specific world communities.

Ronald Primeau, *Romance of the Road: The Literature of the American Highway*. Bowling Green, OH: Bowling Green State University Popular Press, 1996.

English professor Primeau discusses how travel (generally) and the roadway (specifically) have shaped American mythology and literature. Primeau looks at the road as a symbol of discontent in fiction and nonfiction narratives that range from the journals of Lewis and Clark to Tom Robbins's *Even Cowgirls Get the Blues*. Yet while discontent may compel people to take to the road, Primeau concludes that road travel is a form of pilgrimage that brings Americans to a deeper understanding of themselves and of shared cultural values.

Virginia Scharff, *Taking the Wheel: Women and the Coming of the Motor Age*. New York: Free Press, 1991.

Scharff explores the ways in which women consumers have helped shaped the auto industry. She looks at how advertisers were quick to pick up on the interests of women drivers and how the industry eventually conceded to women's concerns over safety and comfort in an effort to increase auto sales. Scharff also discusses the way women's lives have been changed by embracing the freedom and convenience offered by the automobile.

L.J.K. Setright, *Drive On! A Social History of the Motor Car.* London: Granta, 2004.

> Written by a well-known car critic, this work looks at the history of the automobile and the way in which its design and use have shaped and responded to consumer desires. Setright's witty writing style is appealing, and it never detracts from the factual history. It also allows the author to delve into topics such as road fashions and tourism in colorful yet informative ways.

Web Sites

The Auto Channel, www.theautochannel.com/mania/industry.orig/history.

> Although this Web site is devoted to industry news and aimed at car enthusiasts, one section contains a brief history of the automobile and the rise of the major automakers in the United States. The information is somewhat sketchy, but it is a good place to start for those wishing to put automotive history in its proper chronology and context.

Automobile History at About.com, http://inventors.about.com/library/inventors/blcar.htm.

> This encyclopedic Web site gives basic background on the early development of the automobile in Europe and America. It includes the stories of automotive pioneers and the initial vehicles that they produced. There are also links to useful time lines of automotive history. Related links lead to a discussion of road building in America and the layout and workings of internal combustion engines.

Petersen Automotive Museum, www.petersen.org.

> A well-known Los Angeles auto museum's Web site has some online exhibits that offer pictures and some information on various aspects of auto history. Most of the exhibits feature uniquely fast or stylish experiments in auto making, but the images and accompanying text provide glimpses at elements of auto history that are not prominent in most book overviews.

INDEX

Leone, Sergio, 131
Leslie, Roy, 66, 67
Levitt, William, 19
Levittowns, 19–20
Lewis, David L., 46, 49
Liebs, Chester H., 53
Lindbergh, Charles, 99
literature, of the road, 133–34
Little Chef Drive-In, 152–53
Little Richard, 122, 126
Los Angeles Times (newspaper), 69
Lost Highways: An Illustrated History of Road Movies (Sargeant and Wilson), 129
Lucas, George, 132
Lynch, David, 135
Lynd, Helen, 26, 31–32, 33, 34, 45, 46, 54
Lynd, Robert, 26, 31–32, 33, 34, 45, 46, 54

MacDonald, Earl R., 149
Margolies, John, 138
Martin, P.E., 113
Martinez, Ricardo, 60, 61
Martinson, Leslie, 132
mass production
  effects of
    on consumption, 34
    economic, 16
    social, 116
    on workers, 115–16
  Henry Ford on, 114–15
  Henry Ford's work in, 12
  was not unique, 110–11
"Maybellene" (song), 124–25
McClenahan, Bessie Averne, 55
McDonald, Maurice, 17, 151
McDonald, Richard, 17, 151
McDonald's restaurants, 17
Meany, Ray, 160
media, exaggeration of road rage by, 57
Merle's Drive-In, 148
Merry Pranksters, 133–34
Meston, Stanley, 151
Meyers, Bruce, 79

Middletown (Lynd and Lynd), 26, 32
Middletown in Transition (Lynd and Lynd), 33
migrant labor, 36
Miller, George, 131
Mini Cooper, 84
Model A (Ford Motor Company), 15
Model T (Ford Motor Company), 12–13, 47, 108, 111
  as social equalizer, 13–14
Morris Minor, 83
Motor Trend (magazine), 49, 76
movies. *See* road movies
movie theaters, drive-in, 48–49
Murphy, Walter, 74
Murray, David, 60
muscle cars, 87–89
Mustang (Ford Motor Company), 87
My Life and Work (Henry Ford), 113
My Philosophy of Industry (Henry Ford), 113

Nader, Ralph, 20–21, 80, 86
"Nadine" (song), 125
National Association of Stock Car Automobile Racing (NASCAR)
  corporate sponsorship of, 106
  as cultural ritual, 98
  formation of, 96
  heroes of, 100–101
  origins of, 101–103
  Pontiac muscle cars and, 88
  racing, 96
National Highway Traffic Safety Administration (NHTSA), 60–61
National Hot Rod Association (NHRA), 68, 92
  first drag races organized by, 71–73
National Resources Committee, 28
National Restaurant Association, 146
Neblett, Liz, 61
Needham, Hal, 131
neighbors/neighborhoods, cars and changes in, 54–55